Stalking the Caravan

La Plata Books
Copyright © 2014 by Terrence M. Burke

Edited by Andrea D. Maraska, M.Ed.
admaraska@msn.com

ISBN 978-0-9960045-0-3
La Plata Books
361 S. Camino del Rio, Suite 103
Durango, CO 81303

Cataloging-in-Publication Data is on file with the Library of Congress

Cover photographs: Terrence M. Burke
Interior photographs: Terrence M. Burke, except where credited otherwise
Cover and book design: Isaac Hernández/IsaacHernandez.com

Manufactured in the United States of America
First Printing: May 2014

Stalking the Caravan
A Drug Agent in Afghanistan
1971–1973

Terrence M. Burke

La Plata Books
DURANGO, COLORADO

Also by Terrence M. Burke

Stories from The Secret War: CIA Special Ops in Laos

Dedicated to Ambassador Robert E. Neumann

America is blessed to have had Robert E. Neumann become a U.S. Citizen after surviving Nazi concentration camps at Buchenwald and Dachau during World War II. Neumann went on to become an outstanding scholar and professor. This remarkable man served as U.S. Ambassador to Afghanistan, Morocco, and Saudi Arabia. I was proud to have worked on his staff in Kabul, Afghanistan, and honored to have been a beneficiary of his guidance and support.

Chapter 1

July 16, 1973 —10:00 p.m.— Kabul, Afghanistan

I WAS SITTING ON MY veranda, overlooking our small, walled garden. There was enough of a moon to make out the flowering bushes. Earlier, I had fed our eleven-year-old son, Sean, and then sent him off to bed. His mom, Irene, brother Michael, and sisters, Sheila and Michele, had left Kabul several days before. Sean and I were to follow them in two days.

I sipped on my scotch and mulled over the events of the past two years of my tour as a United States Federal Narcotics Agent in Kabul, Afghanistan. During the first year of my tour, in addition to Afghanistan, I had actually also covered India and Pakistan. Now I was having second thoughts regarding the decision I had made to not accept a second tour in Kabul. The doubt was definitely not because Kabul was the garden spot of the world; it wasn't. Nor was the doubt because Kabul was an easy place to work or live; it wasn't. In Kabul, our four children had not had the amenities that most young Americans grew up with. However, they had gone to an international school alongside kids of many cultures, and probably for the best; they had lived where there was no television or understandable radio play. They relied on books and each other for their recreation, but they had a father who prowled the streets of Kabul at night and disappeared for weeks at a time. Their mother typically shrugged with each of my absences and kept everything going at home.

I had worked undercover in India and Afghanistan with no backup. I had negotiated drug deals in rooms filled with heavily armed men who were ready to kill me at the slightest provocation. I had faced off against an assassin who was sent by smugglers to kill me. When stymied on how to get cooperation from the Soviets, I had driven to the front gate of their Embassy in Kabul, and then flown to Moscow to meet with USSR Customs policymakers. I was now working with a beautiful KGB agent to prevent illegal drug smuggling from Afghanistan through the USSR, into Europe and the United States. My time here had not been easy, but it had been thoroughly exhilarating and professionally rewarding. Should I have accepted another tour of duty? This was my dilemma. I poured another scotch and watched the moonrise. I went to bed without having answered my question.

July 17, 1973 —5:00 a.m.— Kabul, Afghanistan

I AWOKE TO THE SCREAMS of Afghan Air Force MIG jets overhead. I ran to the window and watched rockets drop from their wings. "Damn," I thought to myself sarcastically, "who let the Afghan Air Force have ammunition?" The MIGs banked and flew back toward our house; that's when their automatic machine guns opened up at an imaginary or real target. In Afghanistan you could never be sure. I had heard muffled explosions after midnight, but had not paid attention to them. In the morning, my younger son, Sean, and I drove out of our gate. We were heading to the U.S. Embassy, but paused as I watched my neighbor, an Afghan Air Force General, being pulled from the door of his house and then shot twice in the back of the head.

Later in the day, I scouted a possible Embassy evacuation route at the request of U.S. Ambassador Robert G. Neumann, but was stopped by a roadblock of tanks pointing their barrels at my vehicle. While trying to get back to our home that night, Sean and I were forced from my jeep at gunpoint and tracked at an intersection by a Russian-built tank.

July17, 1973 —10:00 p.m.

AFTER A LONG 24 HOURS, I was once again sitting on my veranda, overlooking our small, walled garden. The moon was back up there in the sky. Again, I had fed our son, Sean, and then sent this very tired and traumatized eleven-year-old to bed. The significant difference from the previous night was the intermittent automatic weapons fire that could be heard coming from various directions across Kabul.

I sipped on my scotch and mulled over the events of this long, eventful day. Yes, I had made the right decision about ending my time in Afghanistan. We are out of here!

Chapter 2

IN OCTOBER OF 1971, THE four Burke children and their parents were leaving the palm lined streets and nearby sandy beaches of Hollywood, Florida. We were flying halfway around the world to Kabul, Afghanistan.

The next two years were going to be quite an adventure. Being somewhat aware of the challenges that taking up life in Kabul would bring, my wife and I decided to break up the trip. We'd let the kids see some of Europe along the way.

We had been in Florida for less than a year on my first assignment with the Federal Bureau of Narcotics and Dangerous Drugs (BNDD), the precursor to the Drug Enforcement Administration (DEA). The BNDD was now responding to President Richard Nixon's directive to increase its overseas presence immediately. Although I had only been with BNDD for a short time, I had acquired ten years of international service experience from my previous tours with the Central Intelligence Agency (CIA) in Southeast Asia. I had also been stationed in Italy as a U.S. Marine. BNDD had decided to draw upon my experience in order to comply with the President's mandate.

From Florida, my family flew to Madrid, rented a car, and drove to the eastern coast of Spain. We headed north, crossing into France, and were able to visit an old CIA colleague in St. Jean de Luz. Returning to Madrid, we flew on to Rome, Italy. My wife, Irene, and I had met and married in Rome in 1959, when I was a U.S. Marine Embassy Guard. She had been the secretary to the U.S. Air Force Defense Attaché there. Rome is also where I first came into contact with Federal Bureau of Narcotics (FBN) agents. Two of them would become instrumental in my move from the CIA to the BNDD years later. A third would eventually become the head of the Kabul BNDD office, where we would cross paths for a short time.

Air travel to Afghanistan was difficult in those days, to say the least. Upon leaving Rome, it was necessary for my family to stop in Tehran, Iran, for several days. Flights from Tehran to Kabul were only scheduled to depart a couple of times per week. It happened that we had arrived in Tehran just as the country was about to celebrate the 2,500th year of the Persian Empire. The Shah's government had spent ten years coordinating events to commemorate this important anniversary. Tens of thousands of the Shah's "best friends" had been invited from around the world to participate in the festivities. We were not among the honored guests, but we looked forward to the celebration activities taking place at our hotel and throughout the city. As we settled into the hotel, the air of excitement could hardly go unnoticed.

We enjoyed the first two days of our hotel stay, but on the morning of the third day, our fun came to a sudden halt. I answered a knock at the door to find the hotel's junior manager, who announced that my family and I needed to vacate the room immediately. He stated that the planning for the 2,500th anniversary events had failed to include hotel accommodation for the hair stylists, who had arrived alongside many of the female guests. Ours and other rooms were being belatedly requisitioned, and we would need to leave. It took a visit to the manager's office, and a lot of strong language, before staff would even agree to help us locate other lodging where my family could stay until our upcoming flight to Afghanistan.

Their selection of alternate quarters turned out to be a shabby, rundown, six-story building in a less than a desirable area of central Tehran. The lobby was minute, possessing only a small desk. There was a creaky, open elevator that ran up the center of the building. The rooms fanned out closely around it. Ours was a cramped, dingy room with only two small beds to sleep the six of us. It took a monetary bribe to have a basic cot added. It was not until later that night we discovered that we were probably the only legitimate overnight guests the hotel had accommodated in quite some time.

Throughout the night we heard loud, raucous laughter, doors slamming, and the constant running of the elevator. I opened our door to investigate what was behind all of the noise. Being a quick study, I realized that my family was staying in a brothel. Fortunately, more strong words, and yet another monetary bribe, got us back into our original hotel the very next day. I was beginning to learn how to operate in the Middle East.

Our journey from Tehran to Kabul was no less inauspicious. We made the next leg of our trip in an Ariana Airlines 727 aircraft. This airline was a subsidiary of Pan American Airways. The pilots were either American pilots or American-trained Afghan pilots. The cabin crews were always male. The front third of the aircraft was partitioned off for carrying cargo. A large sheet of three-quarter inch plywood separated these two main sections with a door hanging from the plywood. One was to board the plane, pass through the cargo section, and move on into a cramped passenger area. The flight was fairly long, and quite turbulent, as we passed over the isolated desert and rugged mountain areas of Iran and Afghanistan. Some of the more devout passengers spread their prayer rugs along the aisle to say their prayers while in flight. There appeared to be some disagreement among them as to the true direction of Mecca because several faced in opposite directions.

The aircraft finally came in high over Kabul, and we could see distinctly uninspiring brown landscape and buildings through the plane's windows. There were intermittent dashes of green, where water had begrudgingly allowed trees and grass to grow. The plane made its final, steep descent once past the mountains that ringed the city. A fast approach was necessary to offset the effects of the strong crosswinds that always seemed to dog the airstrip. After experiencing airports in Miami, Madrid, Rome, and even Tehran, this one was a real eye-opener. The terminal building was a small, sad, one-story, stucco affair.

As we approached the terminal, we observed knots of rough looking men who appeared to be doing nothing more than loitering around the outside of the building. Most were heavily bearded and wore turbans. Their clothing consisted of long nightshirt-like tops, which several of the men had covered with what appeared to be castoff Western suit jackets. Their pants were loose and baggy. They were sockless, and were either barefoot or wore sandals. All seemed to have heavy bandoleers of ammunition draped around their necks. They carried a variety of old rifles on slings across their shoulders.

For some of the men, the arrival of passengers appeared to be their signal to back up to the outer wall of the building, lift their shirts, drop their pants, and relieve themselves. Welcome to Kabul! Irene shot me a look, shook her head, and gamely attempted to divert the stares of our amazed children.

Inside the small, bare terminal building we were met by the current head of the Afghanistan BNDD office, Paul Knight, and his wife, Thelma. This was 1971, and I had last seen the Knights in 1957 while stationed in Rome. The couple had hosted several Marine Embassy Guards, including myself, for Thanksgiving dinner. Paul Knight was a legendary figure in the original Federal Bureau of Narcotics (FBN) and its successor, BNDD. Knight had fought in France following the Normandy invasion. An Exeter Academy graduate, he had obtained his college degree at Harvard following the Second World War. He had then joined the FBN in 1950. In 1952, he was assigned to the FBN Office in Rome, and in 1955, opened an FBN office in Beirut. While in Lebanon, he often operated under the cover of Pan American Airways. He had opened the BNDD Office in Kabul, Afghanistan in September, 1970. In the years following World War II and the Korean War, U.S. Intelligence and Enforcement agencies had a fairly small presence overseas. Therefore, agencies often pooled agent resources and split expenses as a way to obtain and manage broader coverage. Paul Knight was a member of one of those cadres.

Knight had a strong physique, penetrating eyes, and a forceful presence. He was fluent in French, Italian, and German. At times it was puzzling as to whether he was joking or being sarcastic in response to something one had done. His expression was always a slight, mocking smile for either. There was an air of mystique when agents talked of Knight. After spending time with him, I came to understand that Knight enjoyed adding to that mystique.

The drive into Kabul took us past walled villages along the several miles that separated the airport from the city itself. We passed the U.S. Embassy, a light colored, squat, two-story building, surrounded by iron spike fencing. Radio antennae sprouted from its roof. Only a grassy area in front and a pleasant building entrance softened its harsh features. Its backdrop was the mighty Hindu Kush mountain range to the north. Two lone Afghan policemen lounged as security beside the driveway's open gates. Shortly after passing the Embassy we arrived at what was to be our residence, located in an area called Shari Nau. While we came to learn that there were some very nice homes nearby, hidden behind the high walls that surrounded them; ours was not one of those.

Our new quarters was a recently built two-story "box" with construction debris still littering the muddy and rutted yard. Inside, someone had attempted to provide some privacy by hanging curtains over the windows. Apparently there was only a limited selection of one-of-a-kind curtains available. Odd patterned, drab colored lengths of material adorned each window. We wondered if there might be a

Goodwill Store in Kabul because the well-worn furniture in the house appeared to have been selected from that type of reject stock.

The Knights were embarrassed and apologetic. They had not seen the house before our arrival, and they promised to urge the Embassy to make improvements. That evening they invited us over to dinner at their residence. Now this was a contrast. Their street was just off one of the busier streets. The latter street was usually crowded with a colorful mix of camels, donkeys, cars, old trucks, and pedestrians. The Knight's street ended at a cemetery on a hill behind a small, abandoned army fort that could well have been the site of a scene from the movie, "The Kite Runner."

All of the houses were walled with at least eight-foot mud structures. The Knight's house had a wood-gated driveway entrance. A servant's room was perched above the gate. Then there was a driveway that opened into a very nicely treed garden. Their two-story house had a roofed veranda on the front and an open patio on the south side. The walkway up to the house was lined with flowering bushes and plants. Inside was a large, two-story living room with a wood burning fireplace. Off of that area was a den that boasted a Russian stove, capable of heating both levels of the house. There was a dining room and a large kitchen. Upstairs were three bedrooms and two baths. The house was very comfortably furnished. I was coming to understand what being the "senior agent" meant.

Slowly, my family managed to get settled in. There were tedious trips across Kabul to reach the U.S. Agency for International Development (USAID) compound for drinking water, commissary supplies, and the International School. The trips were an almost daily event, especially for my wife, Irene.

My introduction to the Embassy was a most pleasant surprise. The interior of the building was basic, but attractive. The BNDD office was in the southwest corner, and consisted of a small secretarial office, main room, and a connecting office. There was a supply closet where a small refrigerator and freezer had been installed. Outside the office's main door was a hallway that led directly to the Embassy entrance and reception desk.

My introduction to senior staff at the Embassy was also heartening. U.S. Ambassador Robert G. Neumann turned out to be one of the finest persons I ever served under in my 34 years of military service and government career. Ambassador Neumann was from an Austrian family that had converted from Judaism to Catholicism. During the war, the Nazis had imprisoned him, first in Dachau and then at Buchenwald. He was eventually freed and made his way to the United States where he earned several degrees, including a Ph.D. in International Law from the University of Michigan. He then became a senior professor at UCLA in California. In 1966, President Johnson appointed Neumann as Ambassador to Afghanistan. After we worked together in Afghanistan, Neumann was to go on to be appointed Ambassador to two other countries: Morocco and Saudi Arabia, respectively. Ambassador Neumann finished out his career at Georgetown University in Washington, D.C.

Ambassador Neumann's deputy, Samuel Lewis, was a career diplomat. He had already served in Italy, South America, and at the State Department in Washington, D.C. Lewis went on from Kabul to serve from 1977-1985 as Ambassador to Israel. He was the key negotiator for the United States at the Camp David Peace Talks that resulted in the historic treaty between Israel and Egypt.

After a whirlwind of introductions, it was time to settle in and learn the obstacles with which we were faced. My first lesson was to learn that my selection to Kabul had been a very practical application by BNDD management. Paul Knight was developing national intelligence as well as heading up the BNDD office. Because I had had continuous "Top Secret" security clearances, and understood the intelligence business, Knight would not need to cover sensitive material on his desk every time I walked into his office. Nor would he need to tell me anything more than, "I need to leave for a few hours," or "I will not be available to assist on a surveillance mission."

Two events clearly confirmed that my new mentor had a most unusual sense of humor. The first occurred while driving in Kabul with Knight in the passenger seat of our jeep. Kabul attracted many "world travelers," who were primarily young people from the United States and Europe. They made tortuous trips from Europe, often in Volkswagen Kombi vans. Most of these "world travelers," avowed to seek whatever enlightenment they thought Afghanistan offered. That "enlightenment" usually came in the form of cheap, powerful, illegal drugs.

As Knight and I drove down a quiet street shortly after my arrival, we passed a tall, young man of a most remarkable appearance. It was not the threadbare old coat he wore that drew our attention, but the largest afro hairdo I had ever seen. In Miami, I had worked with an African-American agent, Forest Beverly, who could "zap" his hair to amazing heights. But this fellow was white, and the high crown over his head was a bright glowing blonde. This afro surpassed anything Forest Beverly could have ever imagined. The man became aware of our stares in his direction and quickly brought up his right hand to flip us "the bird."

"Stop; turn around!" Knight ordered. As I pulled up next to the man, he continued to hold his hand in the "bird flip" position. Knight got out of the Jeep, as did I, and approached the man, who uttered something in German. Knowing that Knight spoke fluent German, I was surprised to hear him quietly speak to this man in English. Knight told the man to extend his right hand. Foolishly, the young man did so. I could see Knight slip his fingers in a position where his middle finger crossed this man's middle finger from below, creating a fulcrum. "There is something wrong with your finger," Knight told the young man. "No there isn't," the man replied in heavily accented English. "Yes there is," said Knight, as he applied sudden, sharp pressure between his offsetting fingers and the man's middle finger. The finger bone snapped. "Your finger is broken; you had better have it tended to." As we got back in our Jeep, I glanced back at the ashen-faced man staring at his limp finger. I wondered to myself where Knight had learned that one.

The second event that revealed Knight's unique sense of humor came in the form of a visit from our BNDD Regional Director. BNDD was trying to meet the new international directives from the Nixon White House. For reasons that made no sense, a Middle East Regional Director's office was established in the capital city of Ankara, Turkey. Ankara was not the modern city that it is today. Sitting within a bowl, and surrounded by a ring of mountains that trapped the black residue of coal burning stoves, the State Department had actually warned employees that their children could not live through a tour in Ankara without suffering harm to their lungs. A clean white shirt, donned in the morning, would have dirty black rings below the jacket cuffs by noon.

Likely in an effort to escape the noxious Ankara coal dust, our BNDD Regional Director sent Knight a message advising that he was coming to visit Kabul. The Director wanted to determine why BNDD had an office in an even less desirable location than Ankara. Apparently, Knight and the Director had not enjoyed the most cordial relationship up to this point. The Director was a serious, straightforward BNDD manager and could not figure out why Knight appeared to be working for him only part-time. This issue was exacerbated by the fact that we had just been informed Knight would be leaving Kabul to become the BNDD Regional Director for Europe. Knight would soon be stationed in Paris, France. This was a much more prestigious position than our Director's, who must have felt a bit miffed that his subordinate was passing him over.

Our BNDD Director had just endured the typical, bumpy, windy landing at the airport in Kabul, and he did not arrive in the happiest mood. I had never met him, but came to know that this was a fairly typical disposition for him. The Director had foretold that he would be spending several days performing a detailed examination of our office's operation, but Knight had plans to the contrary.

While driving from the airport to the U.S. Embassy, Knight suddenly turned off of the main road. We were now on a very rough, dusty road heading toward a large open plain along the muddy Kabul River. It was Wednesday, the day of the "camel bazaar." This was a weekly event wherein hundreds, if not thousands, of camels and sheep were brought for sale and trading. Afghan nomads from the deserts and mountains congregated in an effort to out-cheat each other over their livestock. Knight pulled into the center of this dusty mayhem and ordered me to come with him. "We have to talk to that fellow over there," he told the Director. "He just brought a load of opium from the Helmand Valley, and we are trying to recruit him as an informant." Knight was pointing at one of the camel herders, someone he had actually never met.

Meanwhile, the BNDD Director found himself alone and trapped in a vehicle that was quickly surrounded by a crowd of curious herders and camel jockeys, who knocked on the car windows demanding some sort of financial contribution from the Director for his having parked on their turf. Knight took his time speaking gibberish to the stranger he had pointed out as his informant candidate. After about twenty minutes of this, we returned to the car. We shoved the curious aside and joined a sweating, unhappy Director.

We then drove into Kabul. There we visited the worst of the outdoor bazaars, featuring beef and sheep carcasses hanging from hooks. While all of the carcasses appeared to be black; we showed the Director that they were, instead, covered by a thick coating of black flies. If you brushed enough of the flies aside, you might be able to see how fresh the meat was. I was catching onto Knight's "Kabul Indoctrination Program." Following his lead, I asked Knight to stop alongside the road as we approached my house, which was where the Director would be my guest that night. Knight did not want the Director to see his own, much more comfortable, quarters.

There were no sewers in Kabul. The toilets and home water systems emptied out of houses and ran down ditches that paralleled the roads, into small streams known as "jubes." People could be seen bathing in these meager streams. Downstream from the bathers, I spotted a vendor who had unloaded his split fertilizer sack of freshly dug carrots from his donkey. He placed these in the stream and was busy washing the dirt off of them. Following Knight's lead, I jumped out, approached the man, and made some nonsensical statement to him. He responded in similar fashion. I returned to the car, and announced that my wife had already purchased the carrots that would be part of our dinner that night. They would complement the beef we had bought from the market we had just visited.

That evening, I watched the professed-to-be hungry Director push his carrots and beef (that had actually come from the Embassy's tiny commissary) around his plate, barely taking a bite. He announced that it had been a long day, and he wished to retire early. As he said "Goodnight," I handed him a bottle of Coca-Cola. "What is this for," he asked. "For brushing your teeth," I replied tongue in cheek.

Early the next morning, I answered the Director's frantic knock on our bedroom door. "You have to get me to the airport right away. I have just received a message that I must return to Ankara immediately," he announced. I marveled at his communication system. We did not even have a telephone, so it was unclear how he had received this message. But he was the boss. I got him to the Kabul airport and bribed his way onto the first flight out. Knight did not appear to be surprised when I arrived at the Embassy that morning without our boss. He went about cancelling the appointments we had made earlier for the Director. Our boss did not return to Kabul over the next two years.

Chapter 3

As I was getting my bearings around Kabul, I was also finding out how the Afghan Law Enforcement and Judicial Systems operated. My education also included assessing the role of the BNDD office. Our BNDD head, Paul Knight, had not been here long himself, and had concentrated on developing intelligence related to the overall Afghan illegal drug trade. Knight's impending assignment to Paris required a trip to Washington, D.C., and then making a stop in Paris on his way back. I was left in charge.

In early December, I was made aware that a U.S. Customs informant, Owen Caldwell, was arriving in Kabul. He was to act as a courier looking to smuggle high potency liquid hashish from Afghanistan to California. I located the Kabul hotel where Caldwell had checked in. He was to receive the hashish that afternoon. I instructed him to leave his window shutters open. I then entered a shed in the courtyard outside Caldwell's hotel room and waited. After an hour, I observed Caldwell open his door and welcome a Caucasian male who was carrying a small gym bag. I watched while the man, later identified as Alexander Kulick, took a white vest-type garment from the bag. He assisted Caldwell in trying it on. Caldwell then placed his winter coat over the vest. They then reversed the process. Kulick left the bag and vest behind with Caldwell.

After Kulick left the hotel in a taxicab, I joined Caldwell in his room. He showed me the ins and outs of the vest. It had been created with individual plastic pockets that were filled with liquid hashish and sealed. Caldwell was a mature man in his sixties. Kulick had assured Caldwell that because of his age and appearance, the authorities would never suspect him to be smuggling drugs. Kulick had provided Caldwell with an airline ticket for a flight to Europe the next day, and had given him another ticket for the flight from Europe to California. Kulick told Caldwell he would also be at the airport in the morning, and that they would be boarding the same airplane.

I took possession of the bag and vest and left the hotel. Knight had returned from Paris that day. He contacted the Afghan Police Commandant, Major Omar Askarzoi to ask for his cooperation in making an arrest. Although a confidant of Knight's, Askarzoi was very nervous about cooperating. He finally agreed to help as a "farewell" gesture to Knight.

I went back to Caldwell's hotel very early the next morning. I returned the vest and bag to him, and then instructed him as to our game plan. I then followed his taxi to the airport. I had him check in for his flight early, and told him to not to wear the vest, but to leave it in the bag. As instructed, Caldwell loitered in the crowd. We observed Kulick enter the building and hand over his passport and flight ticket. The airlines agent then passed these documents, through an opening in the wall, to the customs agent on the far side. According to strict procedure, once a person had surrendered those documents, there was no turning back.

Caldwell's instructions were to walk up behind Kulick, hand him the bag and tell him, "I can't go through with it." Having previously surrendered his travel documents, Caldwell was then required to go through the door. He would pass the customs area and board his flight. He almost got it right. He came up behind Kulick, dropped the bag to the floor, and said nothing. He then bolted for the departure door. Kulick saw neither Caldwell, nor the bag that had been dropped behind him. Kulick finished his airline ticket processing and began to walk toward the departure door. "Damn!" I thought. I quickly stepped forward and tapped Kulick on the shoulder before he reached the door. I said, "Excuse me, I think you left your bag." Seeing and recognizing his sport bag, Kulick instinctively stopped and walked back. He picked up the bag and headed for the departure door.

Wearing civilian clothes, Police Commandant Askarzoi and his men had been waiting in the crowd near the counter. They stepped forward and arrested a very shocked

Kulick. En route to police headquarters, Kulick unsuc-cessfully attempted to bribe Askarzoi. When that failed, he told a story. He claimed that a colleague, John Might, had provided him with the hashish before leaving Kabul. Might allegedly intended to meet up with Kulick in San Clemente, California.

The police turned Kulick's belongings over to me, and my search provided valuable intelligence. A bill of lading identified the shipment of a 154-pound trunk from Kulick; it was addressed to a David Kulick in Carlsbad, California. Notes he had made about another venture were the real treasure, though. Based on a tip, I had been conducting surveillance for several weeks on a hippie commune in the Shari Nau district of Kabul. I had observed residents loading wooden crates into a VW van in the early morn-ing hours. Kulick's notes confirmed my suspicion that the suspect location was nothing less than a full-fledged hashish factory.

I had to move quickly, before news of Kulick's arrest spread to the international drug trafficking community. I secured the cooperation of the German Police advisor to the Afghan Police force, Paul Guenther, along with twelve of Police Commandant Askarzoi's policemen. The following day, December 14, 1971, we raided the hippie commune and found five foreigners: three Americans, one Brit, and one Lebanese. We discovered 110 pounds of hashish being packed into false sided plywood crates, shoes, boots, statues, and other items. One of the Americans, Joel Coplon, was in charge of the illegal operation. It turned out that he had arrived in Kabul using a stolen airline ticket six months earlier. Coplon was from the prestigious Lake Shore Drive area in Chicago, Illinois.

Coplon was a "stand-up guy," and admitted his guilt from the beginning. His companions did not follow his lead. It turned out that the young British woman's father was a member of the British House of Lords. "Daddy" arrived in Kabul shortly after Christmas. The British Lord met with the Mayor of Kabul, the Minister of Interior, and the Minister of Justice. He was successful at having the official reported amount of hashish reduced. This effort was aided by the fact that 77 pounds had already disappeared while in police custody. It was rumored that the British Lord contributed to the Mayor's and the Minister's "favorite charities." Joel Coplon was fined 50,000 Afghanis, which was the equivalent of $600. The rest were fined 35,000 Afghanis each, the equivalent of $420. The good Lord paid the assessed fines for his daughter and her friend. Coplon and the others had to languish in the Kabul firehouse, which was being used as a jail for foreigners. They remained there over the winter, until they could ante up the amount needed to pay their fines.

Coplon's hashish packing factory also yielded further bounty in the form of bundles of letters from his friends and customers in Illinois, California, and Holland. The letters spoke of various drug deals that had "gone down." They described shipments of drugs that had successfully made it through customs in various countries. The letters also spoke of drug seizures and arrests that had taken place. One letter noted the "cooperation" of Enytullah Barek, the head of the Kabul Post Office Parcel Department. Paul Knight, had previously reported Barek as taking payments in return for allowing the mailing of packages that contained illegal drugs.

In late December, Paul Knight departed for Paris to begin his work as BNDD Regional Director for Europe. My family's life was made easier because Knight's departure to Paris had allowed us to move from our initial ramshackle residence into his very comfortable home.

Now I was truly on my own. That suited me for the most part. I would have appreciated the assistance of a secretary, though. I was challenged as to how to exploit seized contraband and evidence. It would take time to analyze information and pull it all together. For eventual prosecution in the United States, I needed to identify the relationships between the individuals and tie them in with known drug seizures.

Administrative help came through the assistance of Ambassador Neumann. We had established a bit of a routine wherein the Ambassador would sometimes drop by my office in the late afternoon. BNDD Headquarters had sent each foreign office a television set and an eight-track tape player. The intent was to maintain our required level of "continuing education." We never were sent any training tapes. The Ambassador's secretary would call down and ask whether it was time for the evening news. "Yes," I would reply. Soon afterward the Ambassador would arrive. We would sit, gazing at the blank screen (there was no television in Afghanistan at that time.) We discussed what Walter Cronkite might be reporting. We did so while sipping on refreshing martinis.

I briefed Ambassador Neumann on the raid and my lack of time to conduct the necessary analytical work on the confiscated letters. He had the perfect solution. The State Department had assigned a first-tour, Junior Foreign Service Officer to Kabul. Ann Elizabeth Jones, "Beth," had graduated from Swarthmore College with a degree in history just the year before. Following in her father's footsteps, she had passed the Foreign Service exam with flying colors. She had been assigned to Kabul in what was an intern posting. Jones was spending several months rotating through each of the Embassy's sections, learning the responsibilities of the classic political, economic, and consular areas. The problem, Ambassador Neumann confided, was that Jones was bored with her Embassy department rotations. The Ambassador said he recognized our Justice Department Office as a legitimate part of the Embassy.

He was; therefore, offering to assign Jones to my office to assist in the compilation of the material we had obtained.

Once again, Ambassador Neumann exhibited his support for the work of BNDD, as well as his ability to make maximum use of his resources. Our investigation was a new career area for Jones, but she put her energy and brains into it. Within weeks she had collated the hundreds of letters, identified links, and cataloged the results. These were sent to the appropriate BNDD offices for their follow-up. The collaborative efforts resulted in a number of criminal conspiracy indictments and convictions.

Jones subsequently contributed to several other investigations. Eventually the other section chiefs started grumbling over their loss of her talented help. Jones had to return to more mundane duties in the Embassy. In conducting my research for this book, I found out that Jones had gone on to serve with the State Department for 35 years. There were tours in Bonn, Islamabad, Amman, Baghdad, Berlin, and as Ambassador to Kazakhstan. She ended her career as a "Career Ambassador", but was brought back to the Department in 2012 as Assistant Secretary for the Near East. I appreciated and recognized that I had received valuable help from her. In turn, Jones gained beneficial experience and received a bit of grounding in the "real world" from her work with the BNDD. This beneficial experience is not always available to Junior Foreign Service officers.

Still, I had no secretary. This meant sitting in front of the fireplace long into the evening. I used my two-finger typing method to hammer out reports on an old typewriter. I tried to drive home my need for clerical support to the Regional Director and Headquarters by "xxxxing out" mistakes.

Chapter 4

IT WAS QUICKLY BECOMING EVIDENT that my role in Kabul was not just to develop criminal intelligence and investigations. I also had to educate Washington, D.C. on what they could or could not expect regarding cooperation from Afghan authorities in response to the escalating illegal drug trade.

In late December 1971, I wrote a report to BNDD Headquarters on the status of our cooperation with Afghan officials. Our first enforcement case against Alexander Kulick had been made with assistance from Afghan Police Commandant, Major Askarzoi. Askarzoi's supervisor, Colonel Abdal Hakkim Katawazi, was pleased with the arrest and seizure, but only until he learned that the investigation had been based on BNDD information and actions. Askarzoi was taken to task for his cooperation with BNDD. Doors that had opened to us momentarily were closed again very quickly. I was not allowed to interview our defendant, Alexander Kulick. I ended up having to seek investigative information through the German Police advisor, Paul Guenther. My report to Washington, D.C. warned that in the near future, we could not expect the type of collaboration in Afghanistan that BNDD enjoyed in many other countries. The report explained that Afghans were often suspicious and hostile by nature. This especially came to light when foreigners threatened to upset the status quo. In Kabul, it was obvious that Afghans cooperating with investigations could be embarrassing to the police and senior echelons in the Afghan government.

My report highlighted the fine collaboration with German Police advisors, but emphasized that BNDD was relying on its own unilateral development of informants and intelligence. We would be able to look to certain Afghan police officers for assistance, but these would only be men who would aid us as long as their own positions and livelihoods were not threatened. For the most part, we would primarily be working on our own.

My thoughts on this issue were reinforced on January 13, 1972. I met with Afghan Police Commandant Askarzoi and German Police advisor, Paul Guenther, regarding moves within the Afghan Government. The topic was a proposed cooperation agreement between the Kabul BNDD office and Afghan law enforcement agencies. Askarzoi advised that a long, lingering diplomatic note covering this issue had been lost in the Foreign Ministry, but he did expect that it would be found eventually. An Afghan counterpart was to be named as liaison to BNDD, but Askarzoi explained that his superior, Colonel Hakkim, was against any cooperative programs between Afghanistan and foreign countries. Hakkim believed international cooperation brought with it the disruptive influence of reforms against corruption and graft. Askarzoi stated that Hakkim had amassed a tremendous personal fortune from his position as Commandant General and would not allow any amendments that posed a threat to his practices. In addition, Hakkim was a highly connected individual. He was a close personal cohort of Abdul Wali, who was the son-in-law of King Zahir Shah, and known as "The Chief Protector of The Realm".

Police Commandant Askarzoi pointed out the practical and logistical problems that the arrest of foreign traffickers caused to the Afghan system. Foreigners were not incarcerated at Kabul's Dehmazang prison because conditions there were considered too barbaric. The Afghan Police had no means of feeding prisoners, so any foreigner arrested needed to have money to pay for his own food, or to have others bring supplies to him/her in jail. At that time, a spare shed at the ancient Kabul fire station served to house foreign prisoners. This fire station facility was about to be lost, however. The shed was needed to store new fire equipment that had been donated by the British Government.

Askarzoi lamented the lack of money allotted to transporting prisoners to the border for expulsion. Ordinary policemen could not be given a pistol because they were poor and so badly paid; they would sell it. With these daily obstacles facing them, Afghan policemen soon learned that they could actually avoid problems by taking no action at all. Askarzoi and German Police Advisor Guenther noted that if BNDD supplied information about a suspect to the police, the Afghan officer who received the information would likely turn around and contact that suspect. Warning the suspect would allow the Afghan police officer to gain financial reward, which was especially true if the suspect was a member of the same tribe. Another reason the police officer would report the information to the suspect was in order to protect himself against future recrimination in the event he was found to have cooperated with foreigners against an Afghan. Guenther capped Askarzoi's cheerful assessment. He noted that after 14 years of German Police presence, the Germans considered the Afghan police force to be the most highly organized criminal element in the country.

Despite the forebodings of Commandant Askarzoi and Advisor Guenther, I forged ahead initiating new investigations. A source tipped me off to the presence of a number of foreigners seen coming and going from a large, expensive house they had rented. The house was located not far from the U.S. Embassy, in the vicinity of the Ariana Hotel. It was surrounded by a 15-foot wall and its gate was guarded by a local Afghan. At first I satisfied myself with a periodic "drive by" of this house. I was hoping to sight one or more of the occupants. When that strategy yielded no results, I hired a young Afghan boy to help me out. He was the son of a friend's servant. All over Kabul there were young boys with small, shallow, wooden trays. The trays were either on legs or on straps that hung from the boys' necks. The trays contained individual cigarettes that were sold at street corners. The Embassy's local carpenter helped fashion a tray with a lid and a small hole in the face of the box. Into this, I mounted a small camera, supplied by my friends in the Embassy's "Political Annex." I had the boy take up a post opposite the house gate. For the first several days he did not carry the camera, as a precaution in the event the gate guard decided to investigate the boy. That did not happen, and he soon became a neighborhood fixture. He would click away at every arrival or departure.

It became obvious that these were not "world travelers," the typical lot of young ragtag European, American, and Canadian youth on a quest to find cheap drugs. While the target house residents did wear local-style clothes, theirs were of better quality and design. In addition, the occupants were renting cars that were considered expensive for Kabul. I didn't know it at that moment, but I was scrutinizing the activities of the Laguna Beach, California-based, "Brotherhood of Eternal Love" (BEL). This was a group of hippies that had grown to become a major international crime organization.

Obtaining photographs was one thing. Getting evidence of what activity was taking place in the house was another matter. To that end, I had spotted a large tree growing in the vacant property that adjoined the house. Its branches actually rubbed along the top of the wall that surrounded the target house. One chilly night in late January, I approached the vacant field on a motorcycle I had recently purchased. I cut the motor and headlight, and coasted across the field to the tree. I rested the cycle against the tree and used the saddle as a step to reach the lower branches. I paused to check whether or not I had been seen. For safety, I carried a Walther PPK in a shoulder holster. The last thing I wanted; however, was to need to shoot someone in order to protect myself. Even though I held a diplomatic passport, the consequences would not have been pleasant. Still, while operating in Kabul without backup, it was necessary to be armed. I had also ordered and received a special police baton from the U.S. This was a very stout fiberglass baton, about 22" in length and with a 9mm ball bearing embedded in each end. I carried it with me on my climb into the large branches of my "spy tree."

I settled into the branches above the wall and found that the open windows on the second floor were only about 12 feet away from me. The sheer curtains blew in and out of the tall windows. My view of the interior was quite good. After a period of time, I began to hear voices speaking in English.

They were at first soft, and then became clearer. The two speakers reached the top of the second floor stairs and entered a door opposite me. I recognized one of them from the photos my Afghan "camera boy" had taken. Another ten minutes went by, and smoke started to drift out the open door of the room the two had entered. It began to billow out the open window opposite me. The volume increased sharply, and suddenly I was enveloped in a cloud of heavy hashish smoke. It was so strong that it almost knocked me off of the branch. It cleared quickly; however, and then I could hear strange, mechanical sounds coming from the room. It was obvious that the smoke had come from much more than a couple of hashish-filled hookahs. The two men left the room and disappeared down the stairs.

As I turned and started down the tree, I heard a sound below me. I saw a male Afghan climb onto the saddle of my motorcycle, just as I had done earlier. He started up the tree toward me. I was now just a few feet above him. He said nothing, but the glint of the large knife I saw in his hand made its own statement. As he reached my foot, he leaned back as if to strike with the knife. I brought the baton down hard on his wool-capped head. The knife dropped from his hand. Unconscious, he fell back over the motorcycle and onto the ground. I dropped down beside him. The wool cap had cushioned the blow somewhat. I removed it and found there was no bleeding. His pulse was reasonably strong and steady. He began to groan and attempted to sit up. I decided I'd accomplished enough for one evening. I jumped on the bike, cranked it up, and shot across the field. Someone was going to have a hell of a headache the next day. Who he was, or why he had confronted me, I had no idea and never learned.

Chapter 5

IT TOOK A DAY TO negotiate a raid on the target drug house with Commandant Askarzoi. He assigned an Afghan officer and a small contingent of police to accompany me. He warned me to not give out the target address until we had reached the house. Otherwise, he feared the raid would be compromised. Askarzoi had committed to allowing us to be joined by CBS television producer, Dean Brelis, and his camera crew. The purpose was to show that the Afghans were willing to cooperate in the international crackdown on illegal drug trafficking. Brelis had just arrived in Kabul after filming the latest India/Pakistan border skirmishes.

Our arrival at the drug house was timely; four of the occupants were just leaving for the airport. While the police detained the four, an officer and I mounted the long staircase to the second floor. Brelis and his crew followed. I opened the door to the room that I had been watching from my "spy" tree two nights before. The set up in the room was quite astounding. There was a large copper boiler with tubes running to and from it. It looked just like pictures I had seen of a Kentucky moonshine distillery. The difference was, instead of an alcohol product, this rig was liquefying hashish. They were boiling it down with 180-proof alcohol, and had made it twelve times more potent than ordinary hashish. This bust turned out to be one of the first such hashish operations seized in the world. Brelis requested and recorded my comments regarding our discovery. I really had to ad lib; I had never seen such an operation before. He obliged my request to keep my face out of the film and to not mention my name.

The room and distillery yielded some 25 gallons of finished liquid hashish. Also seized were: 22–33 pounds of standard hashish, distillation instructions, a small amount of heroin, and miscellaneous drugs. Eight thousand dollars in $100 dollar bills was seized. Numerous false and real identity cards, passports, and other documents were discovered. Those documents also indicated that there were a number of other people operating out of the house. The estimated stateside value of the seized liquid hashish was six million U.S. dollars at that time. Two of those arrested were named Jacob Martin Black and Saul Anthony Walters. Because of the manner in which the others deferred to Black and Walters, I concluded that they were the principals of the hashish operation. They were handcuffed and taken to the firehouse jail.

We had unwittingly cracked open the Afghan end of the Laguna Beach "Brotherhood of Eternal Love" (BEL), also known as the "Hippie Mafia." From the late sixties, and into the early seventies, the organization had risen to be the world's largest hashish, LSD, and marijuana distribution network. I reported the arrests and the seizure, as well as the identities of those whose documents were taken in the raid. This resulted in an immediate response from the Los Angeles BNDD Office. There, BNDD agents Don Strange, Gary Elliot, and Doug Kuehl worked with Laguna Beach Detectives, Neill Purcell, John Saporito, and Bob Romano. In turn, that group collaborated with the BEL Task Force, which included BNDD, the California Bureau of Narcotics Enforcement (BNE), U.S. Customs, the Laguna Beach Police Department, and the Orange County Sheriff's Office. This Task Force met in San Francisco on January 4th and 5th of 1972 to coordinate their enforcement efforts against the BEL. Interestingly, our December 1971 Alexander Kulick case was discussed at this 1972 Task Force meeting. A year later, in January 1973, we seized another liquid hashish operation in Kabul. Among the many documents seized, was an actual page of the official report from that same 1972 San Francisco Task Force meeting. Further investigations of the BEL connection were to dominate much of my time over the next months.

Meanwhile, the principal target house defendants, Black and Walters, languished at the firehouse. That was until March, when they paid $1,000 for the return of the $8,000 seized in the raid. They then paid the Fire Chief, Captain

Hotaki, a "personal bail" of the remaining $7,000. Black and Walters obtained false passports, as well as Afghan exit permits and stamps, through two Afghan brothers named Samatan and Torjan. Samatan owned the "Clean and Happiness" hippie hotel in Kabul. Black and Walters then fled Afghanistan, probably to India, where Walters had more money awaiting him. When I learned the details of their release, I prevailed upon Advisor Guenther to pressure the police to conduct an investigation. Guenther informed me that a senior police officer had questioned Hotaki. The Fire Chief had laid his pistol on the table and declared that he was of the Pushtun tribe and challenged anyone who dared suggest that he had committed a crime or wrongdoing. That was a satisfactory explanation for Afghan police officials, and no further action was taken.

The first three enforcement actions by the Kabul BNDD Office had come in quick succession. Other BNDD offices began to learn of our existence, particularly those offices on the West Coast of the United States. They were aware that young U.S. citizens were buying Volkswagen vans in Europe, and then driving them to Afghanistan. The alternate route was to ship the vehicles to Karachi, Pakistan, and then drive them to Kabul. I began to receive alerts from authorities in Canada, Europe, and the U.S. I was provided the names of suspects and the identification of their suspected vehicles. It became clear that the port of Karachi was the most popular location from which to ship the now hashish-laden vehicles back to the U.S.

Someone in BNDD Headquarters had looked at a world map and decided that India and Pakistan were "next door" to Afghanistan. Therefore, it should be no problem for the one-man Kabul office to cover investigations in those countries as well. This person must have been looking at a very small map because the distances, cultural variations, and travel times between these countries are substantial.

Nevertheless, I drove by road to Peshawar, Pakistan via the Khyber Pass, and then on to Islamabad. Once there, I met with U.S. Embassy officials who did not seem particularly excited to see me. I believe they thought that arresting Americans would equate to increasing their workload. I then flew to Karachi where I met with the Karachi Port Customs officials. I described the many hiding places in vehicles, which included gas tanks that had been removed and partitioned to hold a significant amount of hashish and a small amount of gasoline. The tanks were then reinstalled in the vehicles. The Pakistani officials lamented that they had no tools for testing whether or not there was contraband hidden in a vehicle. To help them out, I purchased a very large commercial drill with an assortment of lengthy bits of various sizes.

On my next trip to Karachi, the officials proudly showed me a storage yard filled with scores of vehicles. While there were several makes, all of the vehicles had one thing in common; they all looked like Swiss cheese because of all the holes that had been drilled into them. The officials had either forgotten or ignored my suggestions. I had previously explained to them how to probe suspect areas with thin wires that did no damage before conducting any drilling. The small, thin, drill bits used for testing a suspect area had apparently been discarded. What were obviously the tools of choice were the largest bits that officials could find. The official's efforts had yielded a good number of contraband loads, but many of the vehicles had been clean. Whether clean or not, none were drivable due to the drilling search procedures used. No arrests had been made, as the searches had all occurred after the owners had dropped off the vehicles with the shipping broker and left the country. The owners would wait in vain back home for the arrival of their "thoroughly searched" vehicles.

In Karachi, I also met with the U.S. Consulate personnel. As noted, their Islamabad Embassy counterparts were not enthusiastic about having a federal narcotics agent running around Pakistan stirring things up. In contrast, the staff in Karachi was very cooperative. Arrangements were made to have a young woman Vice Consul serve as a liaison between my office and the Karachi Port Customs authorities. Thereafter, I was able to send her the details of suspect smugglers and vehicles coming from Kabul. This reduced the Pakistan officials' need to drill and destroy every Westerner's vehicle that came to them. They could now concentrate more of their efforts on only the most likely targets.

Flying between Islamabad and Karachi was always an adventure in those days. I came to learn why the national airline, Pakistan International Airlines (PIA,) was affectionately known as "Panic in the Air." The road trip back through Peshawar, the Khyber Pass, and the Kabul Gorge was no less an adventure. At that time, Peshawar was a quiet, Northwest Frontier town. USAID even had a pleasant cottage there that Kabul Embassy employees could rent for "rest and relaxation" or "R&R." A nearby Chinese restaurant provided a break from the Pakistani menu. Liquor restrictions were strongly enforced in Peshawar. Fortunately, the Chinese restaurant would offer Western guests "special tea," which was chilled beer served in a large teapot.

Heading west out of Peshawar, you came to Rudyard Kipling's country, the Northwest Frontier. This included the Khyber Pass and Landi Khotal. Khotal had underground shops that sold replicas of just about every known type of firearm. To the south of Peshawar was Darra Adamkhel where many of those replicas were made. Ambassador Neumann enjoyed telling visitors that for $300 you could buy a beautiful copy of a Weatherby big game rifle in Landi Khotal. For another $300 you could have it made capable of actually firing. At the Pakistan/Afghan border in Torkham, you presented your passport to an obese, pajama-clad Pakistan official in a dirt-floored, smelly hut. The Pakistani border official always made it clear how lowly he regarded Americans. A few miles further down the road was the Afghan border post. It was manned by a couple of soldiers who rarely made note of one's passing.

Once in Afghanistan, the road wove through fertile areas around Jalalabad and then began the twisting climb up through Surubi Pass and the Kabul Gorge. It was in this mountainous area of breathtakingly sheer drop offs that the drive became increasingly dangerous. Rounding a curve, you could suddenly be confronted by men with a blood-filled sheep carcass. As you passed, they would throw the carcass in front of your vehicle. If you hit it, the front of your vehicle would be covered with blood, but you would not dare stop. A mile or so further, a couple of Afghan Police would be in the middle of the road, waving for you to halt. If you were foolish enough to do so, you would be informed that you had just struck and killed the daughter of the village elder. The policemen would impose a fine on the spot. The fine would be equal to whatever money you had on you at the time. Fortunately, most of these rural police had either never been issued a gun, or they had sold it. You blasted your horn, swerved around them, and kept going. Cleaning the blood off of the vehicle was always a messy chore. On one road trip with my family, I stopped when I saw a line of horsemen making their way down a ravine toward the road. In their midst was a woman in a white "chadri," apparently headed for her wedding. When I stopped the car and took out my camera to capture the moment, several of the men raised their rifles and fired. Luckily they were still a distance away. I didn't stick around to congratulate the bride.

Chapter 6

ON MY RETURN TO KABUL, I was requested by Police
Commandant Askarzoi to assist in a joint investigation with
the German police. Askarzoi and the German police were
attempting to develop a case against Safizadah, the owner
of the Aziz Pharmacy. He was also the commercial representative to King Zahir. Safizadah was the principal suspect
in a German opium and hashish smuggling case. On the
morning of February 26th, I went to the pharmacy garbed
in my "world traveler" attire. I made a purchase of one gram
of cocaine and one ampoule of morphine from the manager. I informed the manager that if the drugs tested well,
I would return to purchase 500 ampoules of the morphine
and five grams of the cocaine. The manager agreed to have
that amount ready at 2:00 p.m. that afternoon.

Police Commandant Askarzoi briefed three investigators at 1:30 p.m.. Plans were made for the manager to be
arrested when he delivered the drugs to me. German Police
advisor, Paul Guenther, was to accompany the police, but
their departure from the station was delayed. One investigator had disappeared for 15 minutes. He was discovered
by Guenther making a telephone call. On my return to the

pharmacy, I was told by the son of the manager that his father was on his way with the drugs, and that I should return in another hour. When I returned at 3:00 p.m, I was met by the now highly agitated son. He told me to leave the store, and that morphine was not sold there in the pharmacy, as it was illegal. He denied making the earlier statement that his father was bringing the drugs.

Advisor Guenther thought it was probably the disappearing investigator who warned the pharmacy. Commandant Askarzoi disagreed. He said he had informed his boss, Colonel Hakkim, of the case between 2:00 p.m. and 3:00 p.m.. He believed it was Hakkim who had compromised the investigation. Askarzoi may well have been correct, and may have earned the ire of Hakkim by cooperating with the investigation.

Shortly after the incident, the German advisors submitted a proposed list to the Minister of Interior. It detailed the names of Afghan Police who were to be trained in Germany. That list was turned down. A new list, with Askarzoi's name at the top, was returned to the Germans. The German advisors learned that the Minister and Colonel Hakkim believed that Askarzoi had become too friendly with the German police and BNDD. They wanted to get him out of the way, and a year of training in Germany would fit the bill. I advised BNDD Headquarters of the compromised investigation. I noted that for the next few months I would concentrate on gathering intelligence unilaterally. The intelligence could likely result in seizures and arrests outside of Afghanistan. Arrests in Kabul, I noted, often resulted only in enriching a few police officers, and would have little impact in terms of disrupting international drug trafficking.

The Alexander Kulick arrest at the airport back in December had produced another positive result. It had given me the opportunity to meet and gradually develop a relationship with the airport's Security Director, Abdul Samad Azhar. This became the most productive and honest relationship I had with an Afghan police officer during my two years in Afghanistan. Azhar was a secret member of the Afghan Parcham Party, the illegal communist party of Afghanistan. Azhar had undergone extensive police training in Egypt. He had an excellent command of the English language, and this made working together easier for us. I was usually struggling to communicate in a mix of English, German, and the Farsi I attempted to find time to learn. While we could communicate well, Azhar remained wary of me as a foreigner and did not want to suffer the reputation of being too close to me.

Despite this, we began to make progress. A lot of the drugs being shipped out of Kabul were being shipped as air freight. The drugs were often hidden in trunks and packing crates that ostensibly carried Afghan carpets and handicrafts to Europe, Canada, and the U.S. I had identified many of the Afghan shops that were supplying the hashish, rugs, and handicrafts. I was watching for activity by Western suspects at the shops. I would then ask Azhar to check the airway bills for outgoing shipments that might be related to this activity. Of particular interest were shipments sent by a suspect Afghan business, or one of my Western smugglers. If the suspect shipper and suspect destination of a shipment matched, I would send an alert to the BNDD office in that country. Thanks to the many documents and letters that had been seized in the raids to date, I had a good list of likely suspects' addresses.

It didn't take long for us to agree on the weakness of this system. Spending time looking through the shoeboxes full of airway bills was not in his job description as Chief of Security. He had many other, more important duties. The problem was that there was no one else on his staff that he trusted to assist me. The solution came thanks to the scheduling of flight activity at the airport. After the morning flights on Thursdays, there were no other flights scheduled until late in the afternoon. It was the practice of the entire airport staff and airlines personnel to leave the airport around 11:00 a.m.. They would not return for some hours. Azhar would leave the shoeboxes of waybills on his desk. I would arrive after all airport personnel had left. I could then take my time going through the waybills. The results of my alerts to officials in Europe, Great Britain, Canada, and the U.S. were almost immediate. Many seizures were made and investigations initiated in each of those countries. I had requested that the source of their intelligence remain confidential. This request was warmly welcomed. It gave local officers the ability to claim sole credit for the seizures and arrests. Cops everywhere love that.

The smugglers began to figure out that the information resulting in the seizures and arrests was probably coming from Kabul. As the only narcotic agent in the country, it was easy for them to assume that I was involved. The smugglers did overestimate their ability to track my activities, though. In March, my BNDD colleague in Indonesia, Joe Braddock, reported information from his sources there, who said that drug traffickers in Kabul were aware of all Kabul BNDD office activity, and that my servant was being paid for information. While I welcomed the alert, I was quite sure Shagasi, my recently hired Pushtun gardener/guard, was not a source of information for the traffickers. He spoke no English and only a few words of Farsi. He had trouble communicating with non-Pushtun Afghans, much less Americans. Although Shagasi would be able to pass along the times that I arrived and departed from my residence, he would have no other information of value. It was known; though, that all Afghan servants working for foreigners had regularly scheduled days when they were required to go to the offices of the Afghan Intelligence Service. There, they reported on the activities of their employers. My colleague's warning did cause me to review all of my security practices. I frequently changed the vehicles I was using, and varied my arrival and departure times at the Embassy. I began to rely more on my motorcycle in order to keep from being tailed as I wove through the camels and donkeys that clogged Kabul's streets. I was always armed.

Chapter 7

LIFE IN KABUL AS FOREIGNER was not all security alerts
and informing colleagues in various countries of drug shipments. My wife and I had created friendships within our
"embassy community." We had met new acquaintances from
the British and German Embassies, as well as Westerners
who were there for business or other reasons. The British,
adhering to tradition, never let the shortcomings of their
foreign posting interfere with the "proper British" style of
entertaining. British Consul Geoffrey Cowling and his wife,
Irene, would host small, intimate black-tie dinners. The dinners would be held at their cottage-style home in the British
compound. The wine would flow, and dinner would be
full of laughter and fun. After dinner, following traditional
protocol, the men would retire to Geoff's small study for
cigars and brandy. There, over a large antique world globe,
we discussed the latest Afghan political events. Our wives
would retire to the upstairs master bedroom, and rejoin the
men later in the study. One of the guests was a particularly
great source for Afghan gossip. Jan Van der Pant, a British
dentist, was loosely attached to the British Embassy. Van
der Pant attended to the British staff, their families, and to

patients from other embassies. He had somehow become the dentist of choice for the Afghan royal family, including King Zahir Shah. In Van der Pant, the British Embassy had one of the best intelligence sources a Western government could position inside the Afghan Royal Palace.

There was also the "mystery couple" or trio, Helga and Dirk Van Der Vettern and their constant Austrian companion, Volker Schmid. The trio was extremely popular throughout the social circles of Kabul. Volker Schmid was officially a member of the German Embassy staff, but no one seemed sure of the role Helga and Dirk played. A handsome and suave couple, Dirk and Helga always held court on opposite sides of the room. Dirk, with his excellent build and fine cut of clothes, was usually surrounded by several women. Helga, tall and beautiful, would immediately garner the attention of the men present. She would stand in a group of mixed-nationality men, and effortlessly, she would switch from French to German, to English, or to Farsi. The language only depended on the nationality of the man who was lucky enough to catch her attention. No one knew whether they were actually German spies or not. But no one cared, as they were such great company.

I had heard that the USAID folks had raised a couple of Western-bred steers in an effort to teach Afghans proper breeding, slaughter, and aging methods for beef. I was able to buy a quarter of one of the steers, which produced prime-grade steaks. Around that time, our German/ Austrian trio had just returned from Iran. They had brought back with them a pound of the best caviar one could obtain. From somewhere, I had come up with a super bottle of vodka. Our international group had one of the best dinners ever at our house.

The Germans in Kabul were the inspiration for a great outlet for the "winter blues." They had located a mountainous site, not far outside of Kabul. There they had managed to hoist a Volkswagen Beetle engine up the side of the slope. They poured a concrete base and secured the engine to the base. With a wheel mounted at the base of the hill, and a thick rope, they now had a ski rope tow. The "ski lodge" was limited to a warming shack and an outhouse. My family and many others enjoyed weekends skiing at our Afghan "winter resort."

German Police Advisor Paul Guenther and his wife, Edyth, became our closest of friends. Their house was located between the U.S. Embassy and our residence. Paul would be quick to express his displeasure if I failed to stop by for a glass of beer on the way home. My wife, Irene, would often join us there. Paul and Edyth were active, outdoors enthusiasts. Many Sunday afternoons would find the Burkes scrambling up a mountainside behind them to explore some ancient stupa or cave. Paul was not a big man, but he was strong and tough. A few years before, he and Edyth had been climbing in the Alps. Paul had reached the top of a pitch. There he removed his crampons and secured them over his shoulder. He was rope belaying Edyth from above when she lost her grip and toehold. She swung free from the side of the mountain. Edyth was not a slight lady. As the rope became taut and Paul caught her weight, one crampon became pinned between the rope and Paul's back. Edyth's full weight on the rope forced the spikes of the crampon deep into Paul's back. Paul held on through the pain and swung Edyth back onto the rock face, where she regained her grip. I once saw the scars from that crampon and marveled at Paul's toughness.

Another retreat for Westerners was the 200-room Intercontinental Hotel. Located some six miles from the city, it commanded a fine view of Kabul below and the Hindu Kush Mountain range to the north. Opened in 1969, it was Kabul's only luxury hotel at the time. Its manager, Alfons Petfalski, an Austrian, quickly became a friend. His cooperation was unfailing when I would inquire as to a particularly interesting guest. This was the same hotel that would be attacked by insurgents just a few years ago. In June 2011, suicide bombers stormed the hotel with automatic weapons and wearing their bomb-loaded vests. The eight attackers and a number of civilians were killed. Three of the attackers were shot on the roof by U.S. helicopter gunships. Back in 1972, however, the hotel was a tranquil place to enjoy a drink and a good meal. On occasion, it was a good spot to meet undercover with a "high roller" drug dealer.

The winter of 1972 was not good for many of the young "world travelers." Most of them could not afford to stay at the Intercontinental Hotel. Instead they flopped in common rooms in such places as the Green Hotel or the New Istalif Hotel off of Kocha-e-Morghe, or "Chicken Street," as it was known. They also rented cold, damp Afghan houses communally. The landlords of such establishments usually posted signs, in English, of the daily prices for hashish, morphine, and opium. Normally, there were too many larger targets for me to bother with these "hoteliers" or their guests. I did visit a number of them, but mainly for the purpose of assisting Embassy Vice Consul James Murray. It was his job to remove the bodies of American kids who had slipped into a zombie veil of hashish or opium smoke. They would forget to eat or drink, or to care for their hygiene. They became victims of their cold, filthy surroundings. They often succumbed to death from pneumonia, or from choking in their vomit. They would be too doped up to clear their own airways.

The Embassy kept a supply of six-by-two foot flat aluminum caskets on hand. The Vice Consul would ask me to accompany him, along with a couple of Embassy employees, to provide him a bit of security when he picked up these kids' bodies. This also gave me the opportunity to speak with the other kids present. I tried to get a better idea of where they were traveling from, and what their motivation was for being in Kabul. Sadly, it was always the drugs. At one point that winter, we had a large number of occupied caskets stacked in the Embassy basement awaiting shipment.

Keeping up with the world outside of Kabul was a challenge. The Embassy put out a daily brief of world events, and there was the heavily censored Kabul Times, an English language newspaper. No television or cable news, that was for sure. We never did see the Dean Brelis report on our hashish laboratory seizure that aired on Walter Cronkite's CBS Evening News broadcast. Brelis had to air freight his film from Kabul to New York, where it aired several days after the event. Mail usually arrived via the State Department diplomatic pouch, and all packages were limited to no more than two pounds. Later in my tour, I was flying to the U.S. with some frequency. This was either in an undercover capacity, or to testify at trials there. When word would leak out in the Embassy of my pending U.S. travel, I would receive shopping lists of from a number of Embassy personnel. The shopping requests became a real nuisance. People asked me to pick up and carry back everything from Pampers to dentures. I ended up having to swear the communications staff to secrecy whenever they received a cable instructing me to travel. Ambassador Neumann and Deputy Chief of Mission (DCM) Sam Lewis were the only two at the Embassy who were made aware of my travel plans. That at least narrowed the list of those for whom I was shopping.

My preferred route from Europe to Kabul was on Pan American Airlines to Beirut, Lebanon, and then from Beirut to Kabul on Ariana Airlines. The preference was based on the size and comfort of the respective aircrafts. Pan Am had the large wide body jets while Ariana had the small, cramped 727s. The shorter my time on Ariana, the better. This was not always possible though due to scheduling issues. When forced to take Ariana all the way from Europe, I quickly learned to get the first row seat just behind the wooden bulkhead that divided the cargo space from the passenger cabin. That row afforded the most legroom. There were usually very few passengers on the Ariana flight when it left Frankfurt, so the first row was usually wide open. That provided three seats to stretch out on a bit to sleep. I worked out a method to continue to keep the two contiguous seats free as we picked up more passengers at the next stops. I would take a couple of "airsick bags", blow them up as though they were full and put them on the seats next to me. As the new passengers boarded, I would hold my stomach and rock back and forth and moan. It worked every time!

The two-pound mail weight limit did become a challenge for families who wanted to keep their members properly outfitted. This was especially true when many kids, including ours, were in their growth-spurt years. Relying on "care packages from Grandmas" back home and the Kabul "used clothing bazaar" resulted in some painful to see clothing combinations for most of the Embassy kids. Kabul was the end of the line for the "rag" industry. Containers of castoff clothing from Goodwill stores in the U.S., the U.K. and the rest of Europe would arrive in Kabul by truck. The containers would be emptied into piles on the ground, or onto carts at the local bazaar. For the Afghans, it was a day at Macy's when a new shipment arrived. Western Embassy wives would pick through the piles looking for something fresh and colorful for their kids to wear. As in all of their local shopping, many of the women wore a long raincoat, in any type of weather, in order to avoid the scorn of the mullahs.

One of the more hilarious sights I saw on the street was a long white-bearded and turbaned gentleman. He was wearing "kalas," the Afghan baggy pants, sandals, and carrying a rifle and bandoleers over a blue military-style blouse. The blouse was adorned with Missouri State Patrol emblems and sergeant chevrons. I often regretted that I did not have a camera with me that day. I would have liked to have sent a photo of that gentleman to the Missouri State Patrol Commandant.

Chapter 8

IN FEBRUARY, I WAS ASKED by the German Police advisors to assist them in an investigation of the diversion of medical morphine shipments from Germany. As part of the German Government's aid program to Afghanistan, they had been shipping large quantities of morphine tablets to the Afghan Ministry of Health. Much to the German's dismay, the shipments were not reaching Afghan hospitals. The morphine was being diverted onto the black market. In addition to supplying addicts in Kabul, much of the morphine was being smuggled back into Europe. There it was being sold on the streets. European authorities were finding empty morphine bottles labeled with something to the effect of, "A Gift From the German People." This was not winning many friends for the German Government throughout the rest of Europe.

The German Police had identified a local Kabul pharmacy, owned by a wealthy Afghan businessman named Sahibidin, as the center of the diversion and morphine black market trade. The Germans asked me to make an undercover purchase of morphine. They would set up the arrest with the police. Paul Guenther had to travel from

Kabul on the day of the operation. The other four German police advisors did not have the criminal investigative backgrounds to assist me, but Guenther arranged to have two Afghan police detectives meet with me. They were to provide back up surveillance, and to make the arrest. I didn't know the two detectives, and I was concerned because they were wearing Western suits and ties. They would surely stand out in the rough area of town where the pharmacy was located. I was wearing my Levi's, sweatshirt, fatigue jacket, an Afghan scarf over my shoulders, and a soft wool cap. This was my "world traveler" uniform.

Meeting Sahibidin in his shop was foreboding. It was cramped, dirty, and unlike any pharmacy I had ever seen. There were medical bottles strewn about. Large, dirty, used needles littered his scarred work table. As we negotiated the deal, we would be interrupted by an Afghan entering the store and requesting vitamins. Sahibidin would root around the various bottles and pick one out. He would take one of the filthy used syringes, fill it, and plunge it into the man's arm. The man would wince, pay Sahibidin, and leave the store. I had noticed there was a revolver lying on a shelf below the table, but at that point, I was more fearful of those used needles than I was of any bullet.

We settled on a price of $7,500 for 25 bottles of morphine. Sahibidin said he would have the morphine at 3:00 p.m.. The delivery would be made at a building he owned across the street from the pharmacy. He stepped outside to point out the building. We arrived at the curb as traffic came to its usual, blocked halt. Stopped almost directly in front of us was one of the buses from the International School; it was taking children home for the day. My sons usually rode on one of those buses. Up came one of the windows and out popped the head of one of my son's classmates. "Mr. Burke," he shouted over the din of the traffic and people talking on the crowded sidewalk, "What are you doing here dressed like that?" I got lucky on a couple of scores. Sahibidin spoke and understood only a few words of English. Also, the bus pulled away at that moment, as the traffic had cleared. I looked behind me as if to see who the kid had been calling to. I shrugged my shoulders and pointed towards the building across the street, asking if that was Sahibidin's building. We parted with my promise to return at three. It was a cold day, but I was sweating.

I walked several blocks to where I met with the two assigned detectives and told them of the plan. I would take delivery of the drugs at the building across the street from the pharmacy shop. Then I would walk Sahibidin out the front door, where they would arrest him. We parted, and I went to the Embassy. There I met with my friends from the Embassy's Political Annex. They kindly "loaned" me the $7,500 I needed for a flash roll. When I returned to the pharmacy area at 3:00 p.m., I saw Sahibidin standing in front of his pharmacy. He motioned for me to go to the building across the street.

I entered to find a dirt floored, low-ceilinged room about twelve feet square. There was no furniture, only trash. One naked light bulb hung from the ceiling. Sahibidin entered carrying a small, lidded cardboard box. To my surprise, he was followed in the door by what seemed to be at least half a dozen bad-ass men. All carried rifles on slings over their shoulders. The room suddenly filled to the point that I was backed against the rear wall. They were not a friendly looking bunch. Sahibidin demanded to see the money. I took the packet of money from my pocket, but held on to it while he thumbed through the $100 dollar bills. I placed the packet back in my inside jacket pocket while demanding to see the drugs. Sahibidin, who was pushed close to me, opened the box and displayed the bottles.

My mind raced as to how to pull this one off. I suddenly started exclaiming loudly that he had cheated me. I claimed that there were not 25 bottles of morphine in the box that I was now holding in my left hand. As he looked into the box, I bounced it to make it harder for him to count. I pulled the box back and tucked it under my left arm. I quickly reached into my right jacket pocket and pulled out my Walther PPK pistol. I placed it hard against Sahibidin's head. I told him I was "Interpol" and that the police were outside. I instructed him to tell his men to leave the shop, or I would kill him, and his men would be arrested. Sahibidin complied. The men plunged out the door and scattered down the street. We exited. I was trying to keep the box under my arm while hanging on to Sahibidin's coat with the same hand. I looked for, but could not see the Afghan detectives. They had disappeared. People on the street were staring at the bearded foreigner holding a gun to the Afghan's head. He began to shout that he was being kidnapped. Almost as if on cue, a small four-door taxi stopped in the traffic in front of us. I shoved the gun in my pocket, opened the cab door, and pushed Sahibidin inside. I told the driver to take us to the main police station. Sahibidin told him not to move the taxi. I took the pistol out of my pocket, aimed it at the driver, and repeated my instructions. He obeyed.

All the way to the station, Sahibidin repeatedly told me how powerful he was. He told me that he would be released, and the police would drive him home before I could make it back to my own house. When we arrived at the station I threw some Afghanis (currency) on the front passenger seat. I thanked the cab driver and dragged Sahibidin out of the taxi and into the building. We went to the second floor, where the detectives were located. I pulled a protesting Sahibidin through several office areas and past startled police. Finally, I found a couple of Afghan detectives who recognized me from work on previous raids. I told them I was operating in conjunction with the German Police. I provided them with the names of the two detectives who were supposed to have made the arrest. They advised that the two men went off shift at 3:30 p.m.. They had probably gone home early.

I turned Sahibidin over to these detectives. I took the drug evidence and my flash roll, and then caught a taxi to the U.S. Embassy. Once at the Embassy, I secured the morphine in my safe and went to the second floor to return the flash roll. Sam Rickard and two of his men were there. They heard my story. When I finished, Rickard looked at me with a benevolent stare. In his low, professional voice he declared, "You are nuts." Guenther returned to Kabul the next day and confirmed Rickard's assessment. I turned the morphine evidence over to Guenther.

I later learned Sahibidin had paid a small fine and was driven home by the Afghan police that night. As he had said he would, I'm sure he arrived home before I did. He went back to sticking dirty needles in customers' arms the very next day.

Chapter 9

DOCUMENTS FROM ONE OF THE raids had implicated a luggage maker in New Delhi, India. He was said to be able to conceal drugs in the sides and bottom of suitcases in an almost undetectable manner. At this same time, BNDD Headquarters was considering assigning an agent to New Delhi. They wanted me to go there to assess the level of cooperation an agent might receive. The last time I had been there was after returning from Gangtok, Sikkim in 1969.

The cable I sent to the U.S. Embassy in Delhi regarding my visit had been met with only a halfhearted response. It was some years later before I learned that then Ambassador Kenneth Keating was attempting to turn around deteriorating relations with the Indian Government. He was facing significant issues; including, India's potential plans to develop a nuclear weapon, and their public condemnation over the U.S. bombing in North Vietnam. At a time like that, I can imagine that the Embassy in New Delhi might not be overly excited about a U.S. narcotics agent stirring things up.

The Embassy Security Officer whom I contacted turned out to be very friendly. He helped me meet an inspector at the Central Bureau of Investigation (CBI). The Embassy officer was even more helpful just weeks later when I conducted a precedent setting undercover investigation in New Delhi.

I was introduced to a senior CBI inspector whom I will call "Inspector Singh." My reluctance to name him is not due his lack of professionalism, competence, or hospitality toward me. Events occurred in the later investigation that would better leave him unnamed. I briefed Inspector Singh on the intelligence I had on the luggage maker. He was quite surprised, as my suspect was fairly well regarded within the business community. Singh did agree to my offer to initiate contact with the suspect. I paid a visit to the luggage maker the next day. I mentioned the name of a man I had arrested in Kabul, not as a defendant, but rather as a colleague. I said this "colleague" had been effusive in his praise of the luggage maker's skill. The proud businessman immediately took me in to the back of his shop. There he displayed a number of cases he was preparing for other customers. Because there were no drugs displayed at the moment, I could not give an immediate signal to the Indian police to make an arrest.

I placed my order with him for 11 pounds of tar opium to be concealed in a suitcase. To my dismay, I learned that he had a backlog of orders. It would be a week before he could deliver. I left the shop and reported to Inspector Singh. It was too short a time to return to Kabul on a roundtrip. I was left to be a tourist in New Delhi. Inspector Singh kindly invited me to his home for dinner on a Sunday afternoon. He taught me to use yogurt to temper the hot, but delicious, pain his wife's curry caused. I also learned that the gem merchants of Connaught Place would sell me semi-precious stones at a fraction of their U.S. cost. My gifts subsequently became an instant hit with female family members. I was also popular with BNDD Headquarters' secretaries after handing out large smoky topaz stones on my stops there. Their husbands and boyfriends were not as pleased when they had to pay for the much more expensive mountings.

The week in then sleepy New Delhi dragged on. Finally, my well concealed opium was ready. I checked out the suitcase and then left the shop, ostensibly to get the money for the payment. The CBI officers entered and arrested the suspect. Unlike similar events in Kabul, the luggage maker was tried, convicted, and sent to prison.

On my return to Kabul, I was surprised to see a letter waiting for me. The writer was a friend who had served with the U.S. Information Agency in Manila, Philippines. The lady's father was a close associate to then Attorney General John N. Mitchell. Mitchell was a President Nixon loyalist who eventually became the first Attorney General to be sentenced to federal prison. The lady had written that she and her father were involved in President Nixon's reelection efforts. She had told her father about my former CIA career, and informed him that I was currently BNDD agent. They had concluded that I was the perfect candidate for a special unit formed by the reelection team, and had recommended my name to Attorney General Mitchell. According to this lady, the Attorney General agreed to have me returned to Washington, D.C. under BNDD auspices. Once there, I would receive an independent assignment to the White House "Special Unit."

Their incentive for me was that I would eventually work for the team leader, who was most certainly destined to be the next head of the BNDD following Nixon's reelection. It was a given that I would follow this team leader back to BNDD Headquarters, where I would enjoy a most auspicious career under his wing.

I didn't have to take much time to consider a response. I had escaped from Washington, D.C. and brought my family halfway around the world. I was having the time of my life with little or no supervision. I knew nothing of reelection politics or what responsibilities would be required of me. I penned a very polite and diplomatic note of "no thanks" to this thoughtful lady.

In late June of 1972, America learned of the botched second burglary of the Democratic Election Headquarters in a condominium complex overlooking the Potomac, called "Watergate." The name of the head of this "Special Unit" was G. Gordon Liddy. Wasn't this the man who was caught? Wasn't this the same man I would purportedly work for? And the same man I would follow back to Washington, D.C. as he ascended to become the head of the BNDD? The answers to each of these questions are, "Yes." It became immediately obvious that it was a lot less dangerous in Kabul than in Washington, D.C. In the years after Watergate, when I dared tell this story, my ego caused me to kiddingly brag that I could have changed history. If I had accepted the position, and participated in the burglary, we would have gotten away with it!

Foreigner's WC, Dehmazang
Prison, Kabul.

Kabul Gorge where a would-be assassin made the right choice.

Nomad couple near the Hindu Kush.

Spring in Ghazni Province.

Caravan at rest.

Hindu Kush.

The west end of the Dari Adjar Valley.

Villagers bringing goods to the market near Jalalabad.

Winter scene near the Salang Pass.

King Zahir and Queen Humaira Begum on King's Birthday.

Bushkazi games in Kabul.

Burke family en route to the Dari Ajar Valley.

Irene Burke, Kabul 1973.

Sylvia and Ira Seret.
(Photo courtesy of
Sylvia Seret)

Sam Rickard at the Khyber Pass. (Photo courtesy of the Rickard family)

Paul Knight in Paris.
(Photo courtesy of
the Knight family)

Leary on his return from Kabul to Los Angeles. London agent Collins, Joanna Harcourt-Smith, author, and Leary. London Heathrow airport. (Photo: UPI)

1973 Military Coup. U.S. Embassy, Kabul.

Author at Band-e-Amir.

Author and Ibex at the Dari Ajar Valley.

Chapter 10

POLITICS AND THE DRUG WAR were becoming a major factor in dealing with the Afghan Government. Senior Nixon Administration figures Nelson Gross and Walter Minnick were visitors to Kabul. They said they wanted to learn the situation first hand. Their mission was to bring pressure on the Afghan Government to take more protective and preventative action. Various diplomatic notes, treaties, AID programs, and the like were held out in a "carrot and stick" approach. Gross was a GOP power broker from New Jersey. He was tasked by President Nixon to run the newly formed International Narcotics Matters (INM) Division of the State Department. He operated with a bombastic New Jersey style that did not sit well with the Afghans, including Colombia University educated Afghan Prime Minister Mousa Shafiq.

As an Embassy team, we tried to educate Gross as to the limitations the Afghan model presented. He was not listening. Gross returned to Washington, D.C. unsatisfied. He left Washington, D.C. a short time later and returned to his law practice in New Jersey. This included his usual behind-the-scene politics. In 1973, he was indicted on federal charges.

He had advised one of his clients to claim a $5,000 campaign contribution as a business deduction. He served only six months of a two-year sentence. On September 25, 1997, the New York Times reported that his badly stabbed body had been found in a remote area along the Hudson River. He had been killed by three teenagers in a $20,000 robbery.

Walter Minnick was a twenty-nine-year old staff assistant to Nixon's Domestic Council. He had been there for about a year. He appeared to be more of a scholarly personality than Gross had been. As Gross had however, Minnick exuded a "holier than thou" attitude as to how the Embassy should deal with Afghans on the illegal drug issues. Neither of the well-meaning men impressed the Embassy or the Afghans. Before long they had both returned to Washington, D.C. to write their reports. Minnick went on to author the 1973 Reorganization Plan that merged the BNDD with elements of the U.S. Customs Service. From that, the Drug Enforcement Administration (DEA) emerged on July 1, 1973. Minnick then became a successful timber businessman in Idaho and a one-term member of Congress from 2009 to 2011.

There was one Washington, D.C. figure that did have a very positive impact on the Embassy and the Afghans. He was retired U.S. Marine Corps General, Lewis W. Walt. He represented the Senate Internal Security Sub-Committee. General Walt was a combat veteran of World War II Pacific campaigns, Korea, and Vietnam. He retired as a four-star general and the Assistant Commandant of the Marine Corps. He received two Navy Crosses, the Silver Star, and numerous other decorations. General Walt was known as "Silent Lew." We quickly learned how he had earned that nickname as he sat and listened to Ambassador Neumann and the rest of the Afghan "Country Team." This was in contrast to the visitors who only wanted to stress the "Washington view of Afghanistan."

The General and his aides were visiting many of the key global drug spots in preparation for delivering a major report to the Senate. Their investigative trip was taking them around the world. Despite his busy worldwide itinerary, General Walt spent a considerable amount of time with me. I think he liked the fact that I'd had a stint in the Fifth Marine Regiment with which he had served many combat tours. He was a practical, no-nonsense man. He agreed it was wise that we were directing our intelligence efforts within Afghanistan, while concurrently pursuing our enforcement action outside of Afghanistan. The latter was where we had a much better chance of success.

General Walt was briefed that to date there had been little evidence of Afghan originated opium or morphine base moving beyond its traditional market in Iran. I explained that the merchants of Kabul, Herat, and Kandahar purchased their opium gum from the farmers. They trucked the opium west to the area of Herat where there were middle-men specializing in dealing with the nomadic tribes. They would arrange for an illegal load to be smuggled across the Iranian border, with the nomads transporting the gum. The nomads received the opium and their delivery instructions. As the next protocol, they left family members hostage with the middlemen. The nomads made their trek west-ward across the mountains and deserts that comprised the Afghan/Iran border. At that time there was no enforcement element to bother them on the Afghan side, but there were increased counter smuggling efforts that forced the nomads to be prepared for possible gun fights that might greet them once over the border and into Iran.

The theory that I suggested to General Walt was based on practicality. The Iranians were cracking down on the Afghan opium smugglers. The potential market in Europe for morphine base, and eventually heroin, had increased. It was only a matter of time before the Afghan opium mer-chants realized that their marketplace was evolving. Their future lay in refining the opium gum to morphine base, if not heroin, before it left Afghanistan. The merchants would then have a much more concealable product. It would also be a product that could bring them signifi-cantly higher profits in the West. We had already iden-tified a senior member of the Afghan Parliament who had become aware of that potential. He allegedly had a morphine base conversion operation located at his farm near Herat.

Hashish, though of secondary significance, I argued, was important to our enforcement efforts because of the international smuggling systems it had spawned. On one hand there was the drug-seeking hippie who had come to Afghanistan a few years before. He had spent his last traveler's checks to take home a pound or two of hashish. On the other hand, there were also the well-heeled, young entrepreneurs from the U.S., Canada, or Europe who would set up members of their group in Kabul to handle purchases and payoffs to the authorities. These group members would also arrange air shipments, or see to the loading of the hashish in previously prepared traps in vehicles. The land route shipments would be headed overland for Europe or to Karachi for shipment by sea. Another member of the group would arrive in Kabul with the money once the purchase was arranged. Intermediaries in Europe would arrange to have the shipments forwarded on to U.S. and Canadian destinations. This way, the waybill for the latter destinations indicated a European rather than Afghan origin.

This method resulted in less scrutiny by U.S. or Canadian Customs. In 1972, operating expenses for a 110-pound shipment averaged $10,000. In Montreal or New York, the hashish wholesaled at about $818 per pound. On a 110-pound shipment, the drug group would gross $90,000 and net $80,000. In a recent case that was initiated in Kabul and concluded in Canada, two shipments were seized. The first shipment was 600 pounds of hashish and the second was 400 pounds. If they had been successful, the U.S. group that organized the operation stood to net $727,270. I emphasized to General Walt that BNDD believed that the Canadian operation, and the liquid hashish distillery operation we had seized in January, illustrated the importance of eliminating those smuggling operations. With their organization, contacts, financing, and smuggling knowhow, these operations could be converted overnight to handle a morphine base or heroin product once that drug market was established.

General Walt and his two Congressional aides took their time and were thoughtful and thorough in their questioning and note-taking. General Walt could only shake his head when I described how the Afghan Police were drawn from the bottom 10% of the Army conscripts. A patrolman at that time received 80 cents per month in salary. The Director General of Police's salary was $40 a month. The patrolmen could not be given guns, badges, or ID cards because they would sell them. The literacy rate of the Afghan police was estimated at 2%. Their recordkeeping system was virtually non-existent. People were sentenced to prison terms, and no records were kept of the length of their sentence or date of their release. By 1972, the West German Police had been training the Afghan Police for 14 years, both in Germany and in Afghanistan. Police equipment the Germans provided was stolen as soon as it was delivered. After returning from training in Germany, Afghan officers who gave any indication of the desire to do a "good job" were placed on the inactive reserve list. There they represented little threat to the status quo. In the provinces, even the inept efforts that were practiced in Kabul were virtually non-existent. Lack of authority, knowhow, initiative, and equipment virtually reduced the police to a token presence.

When the briefings had concluded, I felt honored to have been able to spend as much time with General Walt as I had. In his quiet way, he projected the leadership and intelligence that had made him a top military commander during three wars. We could only hope that someone in Washington, D.C. would listen to him.

Chapter 11

IN MARCH OF 1972, I received a tip about a possible drug dealer in New Delhi. It came from Frits Flim, an outgoing and always helpful German Embassy officer. He gave me a business card for an Indian whom I shall call Khan. Flim said that one of his colleagues had recently vacationed in New Delhi, where he had met Khan, who was a black market money changer. The colleague had purchased rupees from Khan on several occasions. Khan had asked the colleague if he wanted to buy drugs, and offered to provide hashish or an opium derivative in any quantity. Khan told Flim that he was a regular supplier to foreigners, and Flim thought I might want to follow up on this lead. Even though I had been to India just recently, this lead gave me an impetus to return. Prior to leaving Kabul, I sent a cable to the New Delhi Embassy Security Officer, who had been appointed as my liaison person.

I arrived in New Delhi and checked into the Oberoi Hotel. I gave Khan a call and he met me in the lobby shortly thereafter. He was about six feet tall. He wore baggy pants and the knee-length white Indian shirt called a "lungi." It must have taken a lot of material for that shirt, as Khan weighed well over three hundred pounds. I told Khan I needed to change some money. He agreed to do so, but insisted that this be done in my hotel room, not in the hotel lobby. Once in my room, I changed $100 for rupees. I then ordered beer from room service. While drinking our beer we got to know each other. Khan asked what I was doing in New Delhi. When Khan and I had passed the front desk on the way to the elevator, I saw him exchange smiles with the desk clerks. Because I had to provide my passport when I checked in, my guess was that the clerks knew it was a diplomatic passport, and would pass this information on to Khan.

This meant that I had to switch gears from the story I had intended to give. My answer to Khan; therefore, was that I was a U.S. State Department diplomatic courier operating out of Kabul and Frankfurt. I was taking a break in Delhi because the State Department worked me so hard for such low pay. After a couple of beers, Khan began to brag about his drug shipments to the United States. I bragged about being able to take anything through JFK Airport because all of the Customs Agents knew me as a diplomatic courier and never searched me. I offered that I sometimes supplemented my meager salary by carrying "things" for friends. Khan said there might be something we could do together. He would be back to see me in a day or two. It was a happy Khan who staggered slightly as he left my room.

I had figured that I might be operating in an undercover role while in Delhi. Therefore, my Embassy liaison and I had arranged to exchange notes in a clandestine "brush contact" manner. The first "brush" took place in the hotel gift shop. He approached a postcard stand from one direction and I the other. As we circled the rack in opposite directions our bodies and the rack blocked the view of anyone watching. A quick pass of my note to him took place. My note informed him of my contact with Khan. I requested that he contact Inspector Singh of the CBI and let him know what I was up to. There were no emails or text messages in those days.

I hung around the hotel and wandered around New Delhi. I had already purchased all the smoky topazes anyone would want during my previous trip. Finally, on the second day, Khan reappeared. This time he was accompanied by an athletically built man in his late twenties. Khan introduced him as Raj. I was later to learn that Raj was the son of one of India's most senior and powerful army generals. They wished to use my courier services to carry a piece of luggage to Los Angeles. Following that delivery, they wanted me to travel to Frankfurt, Germany. There I would pick up a briefcase that I would deliver to New York. We retired to my room to enjoy a few beers. I asked what the contents of the two cases would be. With a bit of trepidation, and an exchange of worried looks between them, they told me. The suitcase destined for delivery in Los Angeles was a new product for them. It was to be about 35 pounds of hashish sticks dipped in liquid opium and then dried. It was designed to powerfully increase the normal reaction to the hashish. The briefcase was to contain five kilos of the finest Middle Eastern heroin.

I didn't want to increase their anxiety in entrusting this information to me, so I just gave a nonchalant shrug. This first class service would cost them, I advised. They understood that language and appeared to relax, as if they had discovered a kindred spirit. The rest of the conversation was about money. We settled on $8,000 up front on delivery of the suitcase to me. On delivery in Los Angeles, their customer would pay me $20,000. In Frankfurt, I would be paid another $8,000 for my expenses and $30,000 paid upon delivery in New York. We parted. They said they would need a few days to put the deal together. We agreed they would deliver the suitcase to me in the hotel lobby late that Friday afternoon.

In my next contact with the Embassy Officer I passed a draft of a cable. This would be sent to BNDD Headquarters. It would also be sent to the BNDD offices in the numerous cities where my Pan American Airlines flights would stop along this 9,800-mile journey. It was necessary to get permission from each of these countries for the controlled delivery. I also wrote a message to CBI Inspector Singh, requesting permission to be allowed to take the drugs out of India. Over the next two days, I had several furtive passes with the Security Officer and his assistant in various busy locations. I was very concerned that I might be under surveillance by my new friends.

Late on Thursday, word came down. BNDD headquarters approved the operation and clearance had been received from the respective countries. There was one caveat. I could not leave the aircraft at any of the stops until I reached New York. My "sentence" was to spend 36 hours in a metal tube called Pan Am #1. I was to fly economy class. According to Headquarters I could not use the $8,000 Khan would give me to buy a first-class ticket because that money would be used as evidence. The Embassy officer was pleasantly surprised to be able to advise that the Indian Government had also agreed to the operation. Relationships between the two countries had recently been quite "chilly." The Indians had two caveats. After receiving the suitcase, I would bring it to the Embassy to be inspected and inventoried by Indian judges. A plain clothes CBI policemen would pick me up at the hotel in an Indian taxi, take me to the Embassy and then to the airport. The second caveat was that I must then agree to return to New Delhi from Los Angeles. In New Delhi, I would take a second load of drugs from the suspects, at which time Inspector Singh and his men would arrest them. I later wondered whether or not Indian authorities would have approved the operation if they had known about Raj's high-ranking military connections.

Friday was spent trying to get a bit of rest and just killing time. Khan called and then showed up. He surveyed the lobby and then went back outside. He did not notice the discreet presence of several CBI detectives. Khan then re-entered carrying one of the ugliest suitcases I had ever seen. It had two, large mismatched belts holding it together. That was not going to fit in well with the two very smart leather cases that I carried. I was sitting on a couch. He made a conscious effort to set the case next to me and then take a seat on my opposite side, which was a deliberate move to distance himself from the suitcase. He was really sweating. He handed me an envelope, and I thumbed through the eighty $100 dollar bills. I hoped they were not counterfeit. He then gave me the contact names and numbers in Los Angeles and Frankfurt. His California customer, William Groth, was located in Stockton, California. He told me that I should call Groth when I arrived in New York to advise him of my arrival time in Los Angeles. He would drive from Stockton to meet me, and he would pay me $20,000.

After California, I was to call Khan's friend in Frankfurt and advise him of my flight number and arrival time in Frankfurt. This person would meet me in the international lounge, and give me the briefcase and another $8,000. He would also give me the contact information for the delivery in New York. I told Khan I had arranged to pick up a courier bag at the U.S. Embassy for delivery in New York, in the event I would be followed when I left the hotel in the taxi. I told Khan that carrying the courier bag would ensure my smooth passage through U.S. Customs. Khan was very pleased.

I then decided to screw with him. I told him that I had stayed in New Delhi much longer than originally planned. Therefore, he must pay my hotel bill. That was several thousand dollars, including the beers he had drunk. Khan sweated profusely again. He said that he needed to speak to Raj, who was outside in his car. He left and a few minutes later an unhappy Raj entered. I just shrugged as though, "That's the cost of doing business." We went to the reception desk, where he paid my bill with a credit card. Handy evidence for the future, I thought. We shook hands. I told him I'd return as quickly as possible for a second run. I told him that if he had the new load ready it would reduce my expenses. We agreed I would send him a telegram advising my arrival date.

Once it was dark, the CBI policeman picked me up in a taxicab. I watched for, but could see no surveillance in the hectic Delhi traffic. At the Embassy, the judges methodically photographed, weighed, and marked each package. I was not quite sure of the purpose, as I did not expect they would ever see them again. Singh and

I compared notes, and he assured me that all necessary arrangements had been made for my safe passage
through Indian Customs. This was important as all baggage of departing passengers was examined at the Delhi
Airport. We made preliminary plans for my return to New
Delhi and the arrest of the suspects.

Again, I saw no surveillance on our drive to the airport.
Pan Am # 1 departed at about one in the morning. The airport was virtually empty. A Pan Am stewardess and I were
the only ones checking in. I then took my three mismatched
suitcases, one emitting a faint, weird odor, and proceeded
to Customs. The Customs area was a small, dark room. I
hefted the three cases onto the metal table next to a con-
veyor belt. My two, expensive leather bags were pushed on
to the belt and disappeared. The Customs officer looked
hard at the ugly case and then at me. I flashed my diplomatic passport, gave him a knowing wink and a thumbs
up. He paused . . . and paused. Finally, he pushed the bag
onto the belt. It too disappeared. It was not until three years
later I learned that the CBI had not trusted Customs enough
to tell them of the operation. If the Customs officer had
decided to inspect the ugly bag, there were no CBI officers
at the airport to bail me out. I am glad that I did not know
that there had been no coordination with Customs or CBI
presence. I don't think I would have been as "cool" with
my wink and thumbs up.

The Boeing 747 was almost empty. My seat was in the rear compartment. I had requested a center aisle seat so I could stretch out to sleep if there were no other passengers in my row. I noticed several fit looking young Western men enter the cabin. Their seats were separate, but they seemed to take seats that formed a fan to my back. They were still several rows from me. I was wearing my "travel outfit". I wore black jeans, a black turtleneck sweater, and a black wool blazer. I had a closely trimmed goatee and my hair was full and a bit long. At 6 feet tall and 190 pounds, I was thinking these guys may have noticed me. This was confirmed before takeoff. The stewardess who had checked in with me approached. "Mr. Burke," she said quietly, "Didn't I see you present a diplomatic passport when we checked in?" I confirmed that she had. She asked to see it. After checking it carefully and comparing the photo, she thanked me. She then straightened and looked towards the men behind me. "Relax guys," she said, "He's okay." She turned back and advised me, "Air Marshals."

A little more than a year earlier, Palestinian terrorists had hijacked a Lufthansa aircraft after it took off from New Delhi. The late Bobby Kennedy's son, Joseph, had been on board. Since that event, U.S. Air Marshals had covered most U.S. flights transiting New Delhi. I told the stewardess that I was on a special mission and asked, "While I would enjoy the company of the Air Marshals, could you ask them not to contact me? There might be someone on the flight keeping an eye on me." The stewardess made the rounds giving the Marshals my message. I'm sure they were more intrigued than ever. At least someone has my back, I figured.

No matter how you cut it, 36 hours is a long time to be confined to the inside of an aircraft. Regardless of how many blankets you lay down on top of economy seats, they are still uncomfortable when you stretch out on them. My now favorite stewardess in the whole world did not make me suffer through economy food fare. Instead, she took an economy tray and filled it with delicacies from first class. No lack of spirits either. She passed the word when we changed crews in Beirut, and the new crew provided the same courtesy. The crew that took over in London was likewise very kind. Perhaps the Pan Am Clipper Club membership card I showed the first stewardess had paid off. I like to think it was my "mystique," however.

The first class food was good, but it too became tiresome. Even the drinks didn't taste very good after a while. You can read airplane magazines just so many times. At the stops in Beirut, Istanbul, Frankfurt, and London, I stood in the door, stretching and inhaling the fresh air. At each stop I exchanged covert nods with the local BNDD agents who stood in the shadows on the tarmac, ensuring that the bag was not removed. I knew them all. Their presence bucked my spirits. At long last I arrived in New York. Agents there swept me through Customs and into a car. We made a quick stop at the New York BNDD office to secure the bag in the evidence vault. "It's time for a beer," the agents announced. Within minutes I was standing in a Manhattan bar, beer in hand. The Yankees were on the TV screen above the bar. They were playing an early spring game. I was with friends. Two days before I had been in hot, humid Delhi by myself. It was surreal.

The next morning the bag was retrieved, and I was off to Los Angeles. I had called the suspect, William Groth, who said he would meet me at the LAX airport. BNDD Los Angeles had assigned Supervisor Michael Antonelli and his group to handle the investigation there. We placed the suitcase in a storage locker that was kept under watch by two of the agents. We hoped to get information from Groth about his operation in California. To this end, the agents placed a microphone and transmitter on me to record our conversation. Groth arrived and we went into the coffee shop to chat. I told him the suitcase was in a locker. He gave me an envelope containing $20,000, and I gave him the locker key in return. To loosen him up, I began bragging about how easy it had been to waltz through Customs, even with the ugly bag.

That was when he got stupid. Groth had to "out brag" me. He told me that he had a shop in Stockton. He had started having handicrafts sent to him in boxes from India.

He would go to Customs, where they would inspect the boxes and release them because they were clean. He was patient and continued this practice for six months. He was receiving a package every week or two. Custom's attention to his shipments lessened over time. The agents now all knew him and enjoyed the doughnuts he brought when he picked up his boxes. Eventually there were no checks done at all; they would just hand the boxes over to him. That's when he started having his friends in India line the boxes with hashish. Not content with pouring only this information into the microphone hidden under my shirt, Groth told me more. He had been taking in huge amounts of cash that he had to hide from the IRS. He then spelled out in great detail the process he had developed to keep the IRS from learning his true worth. Groth declared he was on a real lucky streak. Having gotten the information I wanted, I took him to the locker. I removed the suitcase, handed it to him and said, "Goodbye." After he had walked away a short distance, I called to him. I walked over, showed him my badge and told him his lucky streak had just run out. The Agents moved in and handcuffed him. Groth immediately began protesting that he had admitted nothing. I opened my collar so that he could see the microphone. He stopped protesting.

Having completed the necessary paperwork, I was anxious to get back to New Delhi to finish this case. I had been away from home for almost three weeks. My wife knew only that I had left for New Delhi for a few days, but nothing beyond that. I sent her a commercial telegram, "In Los Angeles. Home soon." That was not to be, however. The Assistant U.S. Attorney wanted me to testify before a Grand Jury due to the international aspects of the case. The statements the defendant had made about the U.S. Customs inspectors and his IRS admissions were also of great interest. It took another week of dawdling in L.A. before I was able to testify.

Finally I was headed back. I had contacted the suspect in Frankfurt regarding the heroin delivery. I gave him my flight arrival time in Frankfurt and said that I would have only two hours before needing to board a flight back to New York. He detailed his physical description and told me where to meet him in the airport's international lounge. Actually, the next flight I would be boarding from Germany was not to New York, but to New Delhi. I had been pleased to learn that the German authorities were not going to allow the drugs to leave Germany; they were arresting this man at the airport. Great! I had ducked a trip back to New York.

Upon arrival in Frankfurt, I went to the lounge and sat as instructed. I observed an Indian National walking toward me carrying a briefcase. Before he reached me, several men quietly surrounded him and marched him off. I went to my gate for the Delhi flight. Quickest case I ever made.

Prior to leaving Los Angeles, I had wired Khan and told him the date of my arrival back in New Delhi. I stated that I needed to make a fast turn-around, so he should have everything ready. I sent a cable to the Embassy Security Officer, so that he could notify Inspector Singh.

On arrival, I met first with Singh. CBI had identified Raj and they were quite nervous about his father, the army general. They were determined to go forward with the case, though. They did not want the delivery and arrests to take place at the hotel. They would have the same police taxi-cab driver take me from the hotel to where I would agree to meet Khan and Raj. The police would follow and make the arrest at delivery. The arrest signal was for me to take out my handkerchief and wipe my face. In the sweltering heat of New Delhi, this was not uncommon. Singh said that under no circumstance should I allow Khan and Raj to leave the delivery point before he and his men arrived. Arrangements were made for me to notify Singh of the time and place of delivery.

Khan showed up at the hotel shortly thereafter. He was nervous, as they had not heard back from Groth in California. Likewise, he had heard nothing from contacts in Frankfurt or New York. He was fidgeting in his chair and mopping his sweaty face. I told him that I had a great time for a couple of days with Groth in California, even seeing him off when he flew to Mexico for a few days. Furthermore,

Groth and I were looking forward to seeing each other when I returned with the next bag. As to the man in Frankfurt; the story was that he had never shown up at the airport. I had therefore cancelled my trip to New York and flown straight to New Delhi. I was scheduled to carry a diplomatic bag to New York that night, so I needed to take delivery that day. Khan accepted the explanation. He said the man in Germany was his cousin and that he could not always be relied on. Khan wanted to make the delivery in the hotel lobby again. I told him no; the hotel lobby staff had seen us too often. He should pick a park or other open space.

Khan then left for a moment and returned with Raj, who seemed satisfied with my explanation of the silence of their partners. He suggested that the delivery take place at 8:00 p.m. on the street directly behind the U.S. Embassy. He said that the police did not go there because it was considered Embassy property. The Embassy staff housing was on the opposite side of the small street. I couldn't turn the idea down. I had already said that I needed to pick up a courier bag at the Embassy after meeting them. I did tell them that they had to use a better looking suitcase than the last one.

After bouncing across Delhi in the old taxi, I arrived behind the Embassy at 8:00 p.m.. The sun was still up. Khan and Raj arrived in a very small four-door sedan. Raj got out of the passenger's seat and removed a suitcase from the backseat. I called the taxi driver over and asked him to put the suitcase in the taxi. I started wiping my face with my handkerchief. The only response was that the doors to the Embassy movie theatre opened up and out came the American staff. The crowd moved toward the street, heading for the residential compound. As Raj handed me the envelope with the money, I was almost waving the white cloth over my head to signal the police. No police came. On the other side of the car, Khan was turning his back, preparing to force his bulk through the small door. I had waved for the taxi policeman to come, but he sat frozen in his vehicle. Raj stuck one foot into the passenger's side and leaned forward to enter the vehicle. I grabbed the back of his neck and accelerated his forward movement into the door post. The top of his head struck with a thud and he slid to the ground. I pulled my pistol from under my shirt and ordered Khan to the ground. "Interpol," I loudly informed Khan. By this time the crowd had stopped crossing the street and were standing there staring. "Police business," I told them. "Keep moving." They didn't budge.

Just then a big sedan roared on to the street. It was quite a sight. The Indian cavalry had finally arrived. There were four, large, turbaned Sikhs standing on the vehicle's running boards. Each was armed with a long stave. Portable radio antennas sprouted from every window. The inside of the sedan was so crowded that the officers were sitting on each other's laps. Inspector Singh jumped from the passenger front seat. He had a WWII-era web shoulder holster across his chest. From this he pulled the largest revolver I had ever seen. He started waving it excitedly. I ducked behind Raj's car, fearful of "friendly fire." The four large Sikhs ran to the prone Raj and Khan and started beating them with their staves. Then, Inspector Singh uttered the most memorable words, "No, men, don't beat them here in the eyes of the public. Wait until we get to the office!"

Khan and the wobbly Raj were placed in the police vehicle with some of the police. The rest of us split up between the taxicab and Raj's sedan. As the caravan pulled out, I waved to the American crowd from the passenger seat of the taxi, "Better than your movie, I'll bet." They just shook their heads in disbelief.

I gave a statement to the police at the office. I did not want to hang around. The U.S. Congress had passed legislation called the Mansfield Act. It declared that U.S. law enforcement officers could not remain present when foreign police were using "harsh" interrogation techniques. The police had found two pistols in Khan's vehicle, which was a very serious offense. I had an idea Khan and Raj were in for a tough night. I got the taxi policeman to take me back to the Oberoi Hotel, where I took a shower and had a cold beer.

Chapter 12

NOT LONG AFTER MY RETURN to Afghanistan from India, I received a call on a Sunday morning from Sam Rickard. Rickard asked me to meet him at the U.S. Embassy as soon as possible. Upon arrival, I could tell by his expression that he had some serious news. Rickard's counterparts at the Embassy in New Delhi had alerted him to the news reports of the arrest of Raj and Khan, which had produced a strong reaction in the Indian press. Some denounced the fact that an American agent had been allowed to leave the country with illegal drugs, and then return to bring about the arrest of two Indian nationals. Other reports focused on the fact that one of the defendants, Raj, was the son of an army general, and had been able to escape prosecution until a foreigner had intervened. The American agent involved did not seem to be very popular in anyone's view.

This was emphasized by the news from Rickard's counterparts who had relayed a solid, credible warning that the group behind Raj had sent a man to Kabul to kill me. They passed along the identity of this man and reported that he had arrived in Kabul on a flight from New Delhi only a few hours earlier. The reason was obvious; no witness, no trial.

Rickard offered any help I needed. I only asked that he keep the information to himself and not alarm anyone else in the Embassy. I did not want to be ordered, no matter how good the intent, to take my family and leave the country. That would solve nothing. I left the Embassy and headed for the airport. My friend, the airport's Security Director, Samad Azhar, was not on duty. His deputy let me go through the disembarkation cards that all arriving passengers needed to complete and submit upon entering the country. I quickly found my man and let out a sigh of relief. His age, physical description, and the hotel where he intended to stay were all on the card that I took with me. The Indians were not likely to know where I lived, so my guess was that this would-be assassin would watch the Embassy the next day for my arrival. He would then follow me when I left the Embassy and attempt to carry out his mission.

My first stop was the hotel where he was staying. I wasn't familiar with the hotel. It turned out to be a very small, L-shaped, one-story, cheap hotel with a center courtyard. It did not appear to be busy. In fact, it did not seem to have more than four or five rooms occupied; most occupants appeared to be "hippies." This was one of many dirt-floored establishments that offered only a charpoy bed, which was a wood frame with a woven rope "spring" and a thin mattress. A single squat-over hole served as a toilet for all the guests.

It was midafternoon, and I did not see my subject. I went home, but returned to the hotel about 11 p.m.. The only dim light at all came from the tiny room that served as an office. I checked through the glassless window opening and found there was no one there. The manager likely slept elsewhere. I could see a notebook on the wooden board that served as a desk. A few steps took me inside and to the grimy, worn notebook. My subject was in Room 5. I could barely see the numbers above the doors, but I finally made out his as the corner room of the "L-shaped" building. The "door" to the hotel room consisted of strings of glass beads. I returned home. I had established a schedule for myself for what was to follow.

I did not want to involve my German Police Advisor friend, Paul Guenther, or anyone else with this issue. I returned alone to the hotel at about 5 a.m.. The first light of dawn was just beginning to show. I parked my Land Cruiser a short walk down the street from the hotel. There was no sign of anyone being awake as I entered the small court-yard. I went directly to Room 5. I waited several minutes, allowing my eyes to adjust to the dim light. From within the room came the sound of low snores. I slipped between the strings of beads and saw that the room was very small. I walked to, and sat down on, the wood frame of the bed. The man did not stir from his face up position. I placed my 9mm Browning pistol against his temple. At the same time,

I tapped his nose with a small flashlight that I then shone it in his eyes, which opened suddenly and became very wide. I let him feel the muzzle against his head and then slid it up to the edge of his eye socket. Only his eyes could turn towards it. All he could see was a black hole. "Good morning," I said softly, "I hear you are looking for me."

We left the hotel moments later, after he had gathered his few belongings. His hands were cuffed in front of him with a small towel hiding the chrome bands. There was nothing in his belongings that identified who he was working for. He did have a detailed physical description of me written on a page from a yellow pad. I was not really concerned about who had sent him; I only wanted to send them a message. I had asked him where his gun was. I retrieved it from under what passed for a pillow. It wasn't much of a revolver, but then it did have bullets in it.

I said nothing to him, but drove toward sunrise several miles east of Kabul. There was the Kabul Gorge. The road snaked from the west edge down through a series of tunnels and open roadway. The road dropped 5,800 vertical feet to Jalalabad. It was some of the most rugged terrain in the world. Over a thousand feet below where I stopped was the Kabul River, plunging eastward. Here, in 1842, British forces attempted their retreat from Kabul to Jalalabad. From where we now stopped, Afghan attackers had rained rocks and bullets down on the British soldiers, their families, and their Indian camp followers. Of 16,000 people who fled Kabul at that time, only one person, a doctor, made it to Jalalabad.

The purpose of my stop; however, was not to provide a history lesson to this man on how many of his countrymen had perished in the ravine below us. I took him out of the vehicle and sat him on the low wall on the edge of the drop off. I told him I was giving him three choices. To demonstrate his first choice, I threw his pistol high into the air, out over the edge of the cliff. It dropped fast, but there was not even a sound of its hitting the rocks 1,000 feet below. The second choice was that I would take him back to Kabul and turn him over to my police friends there. I would use his own money to pay them to throw him into Dehmazang prison to rot. The third choice was to hurry to the Kabul Airport. There might just be time for him to catch the 9:00 a.m. Air India flight back to New Delhi.

We made it to the airport and the flight. I told him to tell his friends that the next time there would not be three options. Only the first choice I had demonstrated would be available.

Chapter 13

LATE ONE AFTERNOON IN APRIL, the phone rang in my office. It was U.S. Ambassador Neumann's secretary saying that the Ambassador wished to see me. Up the stairs I went to his office. Ambassador Neumann usually greeted me with a smile and a quip, but on this occasion he was most serious.

He had received a report from the Afghan Prime Minister's Office about two Americans working under a contract with the U.S. Information Service, (USIS) teaching English. The report alleged that the men were providing cocaine to their young Afghan students and teaching them how to use it. It was the students who had informed a member of the Prime Minister's staff of the allegation. Prime Minister Mousa Shafiq had assigned his personal security staff to conduct a raid on the house where the two Americans resided. To avoid having the Ambassador be blindsided or embarrassed, Prime Minister Shafiq had notified him ahead of time that the raid would take place that evening. Shafiq requested that I accompany his men to assist them in conducting the raid and interviewing the two American suspects.

I met with the Afghan team that evening after dark. We drove to the walled residence on the north edge of Kabul. My intent was to "low key" the operation as much as possible. I pulled the long cord that rang the gate bell and waited. A young American opened the gate a crack. He confirmed his identity when I asked his name. He was one of our suspects. I identified myself to him and explained that the authorities were going to search the residence based upon a complaint. His response was to slam the gate closed, hitting me in the knee. His second mistake was not moving away from the gate quickly enough. When I kicked it in, he went down under it. He started screaming to his partner that the police were there.

Leaving him under the control of two of the officers, the team leader and I ran across the small garden area. We went up several steps and through the open door of the house. There I found the second suspect. I repeated my identification and again stated the purpose of our presence. His response was to utter an unflattering expletive, spitting in my face as he came nose to nose with me. I can't remember my exact reaction, but somehow he ended up on the floor. The search turned up the usual collection of hashish, pills, and a small amount of cocaine. The two American suspects were taken into custody. To avoid further embarrassment to the U.S. Embassy, the Prime Minister told Ambassador Neumann that he would not have them charged if the

Embassy would send them out of Afghanistan. The young men were gone in two days.

With the matter apparently under control, I took Friday off. I joined my German friend, Dirk Von Der Wettern, Austrian friend, Volker Schmid, and a couple of others for a day of late spring skiing. Our destination was the Hindu Kush mountain range north of Kabul. We rented a large Embassy vehicle and driver, and headed north. This was "off-piste" skiing in the extreme. The Hindu Kush mountain range is a major Central Asia watershed. Its tallest peak is Mount Tirich, towering over 25,000 feet. Our destination was one of the 10 passes on the Hindu Kush range, the Salang Pass, at 11,000 feet.

The pass included what many have described as the most treacherous tunnel in the world. The Salang Tunnel was a 1.6 mile long, two-lane tunnel through the top of the pass that was built in 1960 by the Soviets as part of a road building project. It was a narrow, high cathedral ceilinged tunnel with no lights its entire length. It provided a direct road connection between the Soviet southern border and northern Afghan cities. From the tunnel, the route stretched south to Kabul. In 1982, the Afghan Mujahedeen trapped a column of Soviet military vehicles in the tunnel. They blocked both ends as the Soviets passed through heading south. The Mujahedeen then set off explosives that had a ripple effect through the tunnel. In the end, an estimated

1,000 Soviet soldiers were burned to death. An untold number of military trucks, tanks, and other machines were destroyed. The tunnel remained closed for a long time.

Now, in late spring, the major winter avalanche danger had passed, and some of the most exciting skiing could be enjoyed. There were limitations, however. You had to get to the center of the tunnel by 6:30 a.m. and could ski until only about 11:00 a.m.. By that time, the sun had warmed the snow to a point that it was un-skiable. At the center of the tunnel, Volker Schmid had discovered an iron door about five feet high and inside the door was a shaft about four feet square and ten feet high. Along the far side of the dark, wet shaft were metal rebar rungs about a foot apart, and extending to the top of the shaft. The drill was to have one of the party climb the rungs to the top. He would then reach down and, one by one, be handed the skis and poles of the party. Once done, the rest of the group would climb the rungs and join the first person on what seemed to be the edge of the world. Meanwhile, the Afghan driver would make a U-turn and drive back down the mountain. He would stop at a point where the road intersected with our ski run path, which traversed the mountain from our location two thousand feet above.

I had made this run twice before, but sitting there on that narrow ledge I wondered, "What am I doing here?" The rest of those in the group were very advanced skiers. I was not. Most had grown up in the European Alps. I had been raised in flat Minnesota. For the majority of the length of the run it was not that difficult, but for the first 200 or 300 feet, it was close to a hair raising vertical pitch. Taking that heart-stopping step off the top and safely hitting the bottom of that face, made the whole insane trip worthwhile. First, you were looking across a snowcapped mountain range below that seemed to stretch hundreds of miles into the rising sun. Second, you were traversing several miles of the side of the mountain. The run ended where it slid under the road through a culvert. There, the Embassy driver waited. The basic execution was to tuck in your poles and your body, and traverse the side of the mountain. My expert companions estimated that our speeds reached 30–35 miles per hour. If your descent became too rapid, you could always carve up the mountain a bit. You would lose speed, and then turn back downward to continue within your limits.

You could make two or three runs in a morning. The number was dependent upon the snow conditions and the length of the ride back up to the iron door in the tunnel. That particular day we decided to hold it to two runs due to the warming conditions. My friends jumped off the ledge on the second run, and I quickly followed. Near the bottom of the initial vertical, I jammed my right pole into the snow. I expected that my pole would go into the snow to set my turn. Instead, the pole hit a boulder below the snow's surface. I felt a sharp pain in the top of my hand as my full weight came down on the strap. I continued on, but took a slower run than usual. As was our practice after the last run, we climbed into the Embassy vehicle and drove back through the tunnel. This time we did not stop at the iron door. Instead, we emerged out of the tunnel and drove down the mountain on the north side. On the way to the teahouse below, we popped bottles of chilled Czech Pilsner Urquell beer. The teahouse was a small, thatched roof structure next to the road. Its only seating was comprised of old rugs on the dirt floor. We paid the owner to light some charcoal to heat the metal grill above his fire pit. Our arrival alerted young local boys to fish the stream that ran down the mountainside parallel to the road opposite the teahouse. The barefoot boys would arrive with small trout impaled on a slender stick through their mouths and gills. We would haggle with the boys and then buy their catch. The just-caught fish were soon cooking on the hot grill. Along with the Pilsner and the local flatbread, nan, we had a fantastic lunch.

My hand was very sore during the ride back, and although I soaked it that night, it was not any better the next day. The Embassy had a small clinic at the USAID compound on the far side of Kabul. It was staffed by an American doctor and a Filipina nurse. I made a call and met Dr. Red Moede there. He determined that I had not broken any bones, but had sprained the ligaments. He put me in a soft cast that ran from my hand to my elbow.

What I was not aware of, was that the two Americans we had arrested, USIS teachers, had come to the Embassy on Saturday, which was a workday, as Friday and Sunday were the considered days off in Afghanistan. They had demanded to see the U.S. Ambassador prior to their departure from Afghanistan. Probably out of curiosity, the Ambassador granted their demand. Ambassador Neumann later told me the two had informed him that they wished to press charges against me for "police brutality." Their charge was based on the gate having come down on the one and the other having somehow landed on the floor (which he attributed to a blow to his solar plexus). The Ambassador relayed to me, with a wry smile, that he had informed the two that they had left their civil rights behind them when they passed beyond the 12-mile limit of United States sanctuary. They should be happy that they were not in Dehmazang prison for breaking the same U.S. and Afghan laws they were now demanding should protect them. Not to mention they had embarrassed their government, which had granted them employment. He then wished them a safe trip back to the United States and dismissed them.

The story of this meeting, and the charges against the two men, spread rapidly throughout the Embassy on Saturday, although I remained unaware of it. I had not gone to work in order to have my hand treated that day. On Monday mornings, the first order of the day was the U.S. Ambassador's "Country Team" meeting. All of the office heads would meet with Ambassador Neumann and discuss current operations and events. Most of the team was present when I walked in; my white cast was extremely prominent on my arm. There seemed to be a sudden strange silence in the room as all stared at me. Army Colonel Richard McTaggart, the Defense Attaché, never one to mince words, said, "What the hell happened to you?" Innocently, I responded, "I hurt it skiing at the Salang on Friday." Their rolling eyes and groans immediately declared me guilty.

Chapter 14

AT THE BEGINNING OF MAY, I had an opportunity to speak separately and privately with two senior Afghan police officers, Police Commandant General Hakkim and Airport Security Director, Captain Samad Azhar. The two could not have been more different in their honest intentions or professionalism.

Hakkim had possibly compromised the Aziz Pharmacy investigation. He had sent Police Commandant Askarzoi to Germany for a year of training because it appeared Askarzoi had become "too close" to BNDD. Just prior to our talk, he had rescinded a longstanding order that had given the Police Criminal Investigation Division (CID) the authority to investigate four critical crimes: counterfeiting, narcotics trafficking, white slavery, and the illegal use of explosives. Hakkim declared that in the future those crimes would be investigated by local police jurisdictions under the control of the provincial governors. This de-centralization move by Hakkim would effectively remove any central point of liaison with the Afghan Police from BNDD.

On May 2nd I had an opportunity to talk with Hakkim during a reception at Ambassador Neumann's residence.

Police Commandant, General Hakkim was immediately defensive. He informed me he had heard that Ambassador Neumann was upset about a decentralization order that he planned to implement (Ambassador Neumann had discussed the matter with the Interior Minister after I had alerted him to it). Hakkim said the order was only a rumor. He attempted to explain how he was reorganizing, but his explanation could not be clearly understood. It was obvious he was taking the authority away from the CID, as stated. Hakkim offered up two officers as liaison contacts for me with the police. Neither officer had anything to do with narcotics cases. One officer, Kabul Traffic Chief, Captain Yusafi, had gained prominence when he sold thousands of meters of reflective tape that had been given to the Traffic Department as a gift. It was intended to increase the safety of vehicles and bicycles. Yusafi reportedly made a small fortune on the sale, much to the envy of his fellow officers.

I told Hakkim I believed I could help the Afghan police, but had become discouraged when cases ended only in payoffs to policemen. Prisoners had bought back evidence from police. They had been allowed to flee the country, and in general, made months of investigative work worthless. I told Hakkim that my recent cooperation with the India Police stood in stark contrast. The Indian Police were not only willing to arrest foreigners, but also their own Indian sources. I said I'd be happy to get half that level of support from the Afghans. I was beginning to wonder if it would ever happen, I told him. Hakkim's only reply was that any police officer who had taken a large bribe would probably have to go to court. This, I thought, would be highly unlikely. Hakkim said he would consider the other things I had said.

There was one change that took place following our talk. Foreign prisoners were moved from the Firehouse to Kabul's Dehmazang Prison. While at the Firehouse, the prisoners had been allowed to leave jail daily to go to the market to buy food and drugs. Dehmazang Prison did not allow those niceties. In fact, that barbaric place did not even have toilet facilities. Complaints from the Western prisoners and their embassies resulted in the Afghans converting a tool shed to a toilet. The prisoners were allowed to dig a deep hole, which constituted the toilet. At least there was a semblance of privacy, as there was a wood door on the shed. One of the prisoners must have credited me with his presence at Dehmazang. He wrote on the door, "Burke's Office; where there's a case, he's not."

On October 19, 1972, The New York Times published an article headlined, "Dehmazang, Called World's Worst Prison, Awaits Visitors to Afghanistan Suspected of Drug Offenses." The article reported the jailing of foreigners at Dehmazang. It cited the harshness of their imprisonment and reported the fact that they had inscribed the "WC" door as noted above. The article also reported my efforts to keep the large organizations smuggling hashish out of Afghanistan from transferring their operations to the more dangerous opium and morphine base traffic.

Captain Samad Azhar asked for a meeting with me two days after my discussion with Police Commandant Hakkim. He requested that we meet at my residence at night, as he did not want for anyone to know of the meeting. Our servant was given the day off. Azhar parked some blocks away and walked to the house. Azhar stated that he had requested the meeting to explain why he could not cooperate with me as effectively as he would like to. Azhar said he had become convinced that my reasons for pushing the Afghan Police to take action against narcotics trafficking were for the good of Afghans, as well as Americans. He felt; however, that officers like him, who wished to help, could not because of the restrictions of their Afghan society. Azhar said he was constantly at odds with everyone, from the Customs officials to the Minister of Finance, and on down to the baggage inspectors. He said the prime motivation of these people was the money available through payoffs, and they resisted any change that would inhibit their ability to amass personal wealth. Azhar said the current group of custom inspectors at the airport, with the exception of one, was totally corrupt. He had requested a change of personnel, but knew he would only be receiving a new group of greedy criminals.

Azhar noted the tremendous political pressure against him. He recounted how, in 1971, he had arrested the son of a prominent Afghan. The man had attempted to smuggle 110 pounds of hashish to Germany. The following night, Azhar was beaten to unconsciousness by six members of the defendant's family. In January, 1972, during the trial, the defendant stood up. He informed the judge that if he did not terminate the case on the spot, Azhar would be dead within 24 hours. The judge dropped the charges and declared the case closed.

Azhar said he knew that I had good intelligence on shipments, although I had no idea of the volume of smuggling going out of the Kabul and Kandahar airports. He said the only drug smugglers caught were the ones who failed to pay off Customs, and these individuals were usually carrying only a few kilos of hashish. Azhar recommended that when I learned of shipments leaving Kabul, I should notify the police of recipient countries. He said that incriminating information from BNDD was considered embarrassing by the few honest Afghan police officers, and it was a monetary windfall for the rest. Azhar said the advent of Western hippies, and the growth of Kabul as a drug center, had brought out the worst in his countrymen. He said that the higher the rank of the officials, the greater was their greed.

In response to questioning, Azhar stated that the only way he could see the Afghans cooperating with the U.S.

Government was by the U.S. using political force. The U.S. should use USAID agricultural and educational programs as leverage. If they wanted those programs to continue, the Afghans must cooperate with the United States in their drug program. Azhar said that even this would have its limitations because the very powerful Afghans who were making their fortunes off of narcotics could not care less whether U.S. aided Afghanistan or not.

Azhar said that he hoped I would understand his dilemma. He told me, "The U.S. is trying to do something that has never been done successfully by any foreigner. That is to convince Afghans that it is for their own good to act against their own."

Chapter 15

WE NOW HAD A REGULAR exchange of information with
the Los Angeles BNDD office about the Brotherhood of
Eternal Love's (BEL) international smuggling operations.
The exchange had yielded extensive details regarding
who the main players were, and the false identities they
were operating under. Los Angeles supervisors, Lloyd
Sinclair and Don Strange, had identified the laws govern-
ing the use of false passports as a good starting point for
obtaining warrants against the BEL operatives. Toward
this end they continued to supply me with U.S. fugitive
identification information.

I made a list of the principal suspects whom we believed
would travel to Afghanistan. I added their photographs,
aliases, and descriptions.

My relationship with Captain Azhar had become strong.
He readily accepted the list and photographs. There was
no extradition treaty between the United States and
Afghanistan. My hope was that any fugitive arriving in
Kabul might violate a local law. If not, I would monitor
them while they were in Afghanistan and develop any rel-
evant intelligence.

On Sunday afternoon, May 7th I received a call from Captain Azhar. He advised that a man carrying the passport with the name of Rodney Parks had arrived in Kabul. Azhar had realized that Parks matched the photograph I had provided of BEL fugitive, Richard Bevan. I had been informed by BNDD Los Angeles that Bevan had been previously indicted on false passport charges.

Bevan's immigration card indicated he intended to stay at the Intercontinental Hotel. The manager, Alfons Petfalski, confirmed that Bevan had checked in. I obtained his room number. Late that afternoon I drove up the hillside where the handsome hotel overlooked the city. I knocked on Bevan's door and introduced myself when he answered. I invited myself into his room. He was understandably nervous. He sat on the edge of the bed, and I pulled up a chair that had a partially open backing. Most of the conversation had to do with my statement that I "had BEL covered" in Afghanistan from dawn to dusk. The days of BEL running free here were over. I told Bevan we were aware of his travel and mission to Afghanistan (a bit of a stretch) and advised him that the police were awaiting my instructions as to whether or not they should arrest him, and throw him in the infamous Dehmazang Prison.

I purposely couched my comments in a semi-friendly tone of voice. I foiled my own efforts to put him at ease, however. As I leaned back on the rear legs of the chair, my

Walther PPK pistol slid from the back of my belt and popped through the open back of the chair and on to the carpet. Bevan's eyes went very wide. He immediately expressed his intention to cooperate with me.

I told Bevan that I needed to check with my Headquarters as to whether they wanted him jailed in Kabul or to be returned to the United States. He had obviously heard tales of the horrors of Dehmazang prison. He assured me he would be happy to return to the United States with me. I took Bevan's false passport and airline ticket, and most of his money for "safe keeping." I gave him a receipt for those items. I advised him that the police had the hotel under surveillance (not true) and that he would be arrested should he attempt to leave. He agreed to stay in this room and await my instructions.

I was scheduled to return to Los Angeles that week to testify in a court case there. BNDD Headquarters agreed I should escort Bevan back with me. We left Kabul without incident, on May 11, 1972. We arrived in Beirut, Lebanon, late in the afternoon. We had to stay overnight in order to make the Pan American flight to London the next morning. There we would change planes to the Pan American polar flight to Los Angeles. I was not finding Bevan a very pleasant traveling companion, as his brain seemed to have been fried from regular drug use. It was difficult holding a decent conversation with him. I had friends in Beirut, and had no interest in spending the evening with Bevan.

When we entered the Beirut terminal, there was a heavy police and military presence due to recent terrorist events. I spotted a very grim looking police captain standing with two heavily armed officers. I told Bevan to stay where he was and approached the captain. I told the captain I was traveling with a mentally deficient American, upon whom I wanted to impress that the Lebanese were very strict. Bevan could not misbehave during our overnight stay in Beirut. I pointed at Bevan and the captain responded with an angry scowl and shook his fist in Bevan's direction. I asked the captain for the name of a nearby cheap hotel where I could book Bevan and the captain provided a name and address. I thanked him and returned to Bevan. Again, I took his passport, ticket, and all but a small amount of money, put him in a taxi and gave the driver the name of the hotel. I told Bevan he was to stay in the hotel and to return to the airport by 8:15 a.m. the next morning. I warned him that I had arranged with the police captain to keep him under surveillance overnight (again, a stretch).

The next morning I waited (with a bit of apprehension) in front of the airport terminal. However, a taxicab pulled up right on time and out tumbled a haggard Bevan. He said he had tried to leave his hotel to have dinner. He did not get far, though, because there were police in civilian clothes in his hallway and in the lobby. They had all stared at him in a threatening manner, which caused him to assume he was under surveillance per my instructions. He had returned to his room without eating, and was not able to sleep because he had heard police prowling about in front of his door all night.

Our arrival in London was on time. Our timing was bad however, because airport personnel who operated the ramp to the aircraft decided to go on strike at that moment. We were trapped on the plane at the gate. The aircraft was a 747, full of British mothers returning home from Australia. Neither they, nor their children and babies, were pleased. They were all tired after a lengthy journey and they had run out of diapers. "Let us off the plane," they begged. Their plea was relayed to the union steward, but he refused. My opinion of unions took another drop. After several hours, their "flash strike" ended. I only hoped it was their union leaders who had to clean the overflowing toilets aboard the planes.

The delay had caused us to miss our connecting flight to Los Angeles. Instead of taking the direct polar flight to L.A., I had to rebook us on a flight to Newark, New Jersey. Then there was a connection to St. Louis, Missouri. The next leg would get us in to L.A. about midnight. We collected our bags after arriving in Newark. I took Bevan into a men's room before proceeding to Immigration and Customs, and removed my pistol and handcuffs from my checked bag. I explained to him that he was sure to be listed in the Customs and Immigration computers as a fugitive. If I did not already have him under arrest, they would have arrested him and he would languish in a Newark jail until he could be extradited to California. Being under arrest by me, I told him, he'd spend the night in the Los Angeles jail and go to court the next morning, where he would probably bond out. Bevan readily agreed. I proceeded to cuff Bevan, declared him under arrest and read him his Miranda Rights.

We proceeded through Immigration and then Customs. As I expected, the agents were very unhappy that I had cheated them out of making a fugitive arrest. I did manage to talk one of them into calling BNDD in Los Angeles to provide them with our new arrival information.

The flight to St. Louis, Missouri and the change to the L.A. flight were uneventful. Both Bevan and I were exhausted after a day that had begun in Beirut, Lebanon. We were met after midnight by Los Angeles BNDD Agent Don Strange and Laguna Beach Detective, Bob Romano. Agent Strange was driving his Volkswagen Bug. We finally lodged Bevan in the Los Angeles jail and headed for my hotel, but the evening was not to be over that soon.

As we drove through downtown LA, I spotted two U.S. Marines walking down the sidewalk. There was a third and fourth man right behind them. From the car, I saw the third man pull a pistol from his belt and point it at the Marines. I told Strange to whip a U-turn and pull up alongside the gunman. Being in the passenger seat, I would jump out. They should then pursue the fourth man who had gone ahead of the Marines. Strange made the turn, and I went out the door, gun in hand; I ordered the gunman to "freeze." When he had seen us coming for him, he had shoved his gun into the front of his waistband. Now, instead of "freezing" as I ordered, he started to pull the gun out from his waistband. I told myself to wait until his gun cleared his belt before I shot him from only a few feet away. Luckily, there was good street lighting in the area, which allowed me to see that the man was pulling out his gun using only his thumb and forefinger on the butt. As the gun cleared his belt, he opened his hand, and the gun dropped to the ground. I then dropped him to the ground and cuffed him.

Uniformed cops soon rolled in. They discovered that the gunman was a 17-year-old Mexican boy. He spoke no English. The gun was 9mm Luger "replica;" not a real gun. One policeman told me, "You should have shot him anyway; we would have backed you up." I went to sleep that night thinking of the morning L.A. newspaper headlines, which could have been: "Sleep Deprived Federal Agent Kills Mexican Teenager Armed with a Toy Pistol."

The next morning I went to the Los Angeles jail to pick up Bevan for his Federal Court appearance. There were also other federal agents picking up their prisoners. While waiting for Bevan, I noted how carelessly some of the agents patted down and cuffed their wards. I also saw that the waiting group of prisoners observed this as well. Some of them even pantomimed the agents. When Bevan was brought out, I whirled him around against the wall. I kicked his legs apart and thoroughly and roughly searched him. Then I cuffed him behind his back. We walked out to the "Wow" murmurs from the other prisoners. I turned and scowled at them. "BNDD," I growled.

At the court hearing, I had to acknowledge that Bevan had traveled with me in a cooperative manner. He had in no way resisted returning to the United States, but I did not mention some of the inducements that accounted for his stellar behavior. Against the arguments of the Assistant U.S. Attorney, the judge set a very low bail of $10,000 for Bevan's passport violation charges. As I had predicted, a BEL friend bonded him out that day. He jumped bond and was last reported to have gone to Hawaii.

The Los Angeles trial at which I was to testify was delayed for a couple of days. That gave me the chance to rent a car and drive south to Valley Center, where my sister lived with her husband and two sons, Scott and Troy. I returned to Los Angles late on Sunday afternoon via a rural, two-lane road that had little traffic. I was passed by a car heading north at a very high speed. That car was quickly followed by a Sheriff's department patrol car that was running code with lights and siren. I came around a curve a ways up the road and observed both cars stopped, partially blocking the right lane. The deputy sheriff was taking the driver out of his car. Because of an oncoming car, I stopped behind the cruiser. As I did, I saw the deputy have the tall, solid looking man stand and face his car with his hands on the roof. As the deputy started to pat him down, I realized that the man was standing upright and his legs were barely spread. He was not off balance as he should have been. Realizing this could be a problem; I put the car in park, opened the door and stepped onto the road. As I did, the deputy knelt down and ran his hands down the man's leg to his boots. At that moment, the man turned and brought his right fist down and struck the deputy on his right temple. The deputy went down as though pole-axed and lay unconscious on the ground.

The man had not noticed me. He bent, reaching for the pistol on the deputy's belt, but I was on him before he could. I pressed my gun against his head, telling him, "I'm talking to a dead man." I had found that a more useful phrase to catch a suspect's attention than, "You are under arrest." I put him back against the car, but this time with his legs stretched and pulled back to the breaking point. This left him totally off balance. The deputy was beginning to stir as I took his handcuffs from the pouch on his belt and placed them on his assailant. I searched the man and put him in the back seat of the deputy's car. I made sure the back doors were locked. The deputy was groggy, but awake. I showed him my badge as he got to his feet. I told him his prisoner was handcuffed in the back seat of the cruiser. His only response was to key the radio he took from his belt and frantically call his dispatcher. He told dispatch something to the effect that he was down and under assault by the man he had stopped. I was dressed in Levis, a shirt, and Levis jacket. I didn't want other deputies rolling up and mistaking me for the assailant. I wished the deputy well and got out of there. A few miles north I was passed by what must have been the sheriff's department's entire cruiser fleet roaring south. Their lights were blazing and sirens screaming. As I continued north, I had the thought that it seemed as though Kabul was safer than Southern California.

Back in Kabul, some weeks later, I received a letter from my sister. I had related the incident to her before I left Los Angeles. Inside was a local newspaper article and picture of my now grinning deputy. He was receiving an award for single handedly subduing a fleeing felon who had attacked him while being arrested. What a guy!

Chapter 16

THE END OF MAY IN 1972 brought some big changes for my Afghan operation. The best was a long overdue funding authorization by BNDD Headquarters. After suffering through my "xxxxed out" reports, they had finally provided me with the funds to hire a secretary. I believed that my comments to General Walt may have spurred BNDD's decision. I put the word out through the Embassy's dependent wives' network that I was looking for a candidate. Many of these women had left very good jobs in the United States in order to accompany their husbands to Afghanistan. Jobs for dependents in Kabul were strictly limited to the Embassy, and the need there was quite restrictive due to the small size of the Mission. The chance to have a very responsible position was a great attraction to some of the wives, but this turned out to be both a blessing and a curse for me.

There was no lack of applicants, and it quickly became apparent that the rivalry among them was palpable. There were several serious selection criteria. The candidate would be fully aware of the sensitive and potentially dangerous operations we were engaged in. It would be required that the secretary not talk about our intelligence and operations to anyone other than myself. This was a difficult requirement as discussing rumors was considered a "blood sport" in our small Embassy community. There were many rumored liaisons between various husbands and wives. Deputy Chief of Mission, Sam Lewis, quipped that he needed to have staff and their wives wear numbers on their backs so he could keep track of who was with whom. I knew he was joking, but we were a small group with few outsiders. Rumors, true or not, were a fact of life.

The wife of one of the military members of the Defense Attaché's Office met all of my criteria. Delle Brandyburg was a smart and articulate woman who could literally burn the keys off a typewriter. She was probably the only African-American woman in Kabul. Brandyburg was tall enough to almost stand eye-to-eye with me. Later, once she got to know me, she was honest enough to let me know when I was screwing up. My previous contact with her had been limited, but her reputation was that of a person whom you could trust. That did it for me. My experience working with her proved me correct.

A negative change that came about was the departure of German Police Advisor, Paul Guenther and his wife, Edyth. Paul had been a mentor and guiding light regarding how to operate in Afghanistan, and to how to deal with Afghan Police. He didn't work out of a comfortable embassy office, as I did, but instead had a grungy office in the police headquarters. I had found myself dealing with one of the Afghan officers on a regular basis. His office was next to Guenther's. One day this officer and I were attempting to discuss an investigation. He had been trained in Germany, but had about as much proficiency speaking German as I had retained from the German course I had taken at Georgetown University years before. To make up for our common German deficiency, we interspersed German with a bit of English and Farsi in our conversations. Guenther had been next door monitoring our conversation through the thin office walls. He suddenly burst through the connecting door holding his hands to his ears. "Stop!" he demanded, "What are you doing to my language?"

Our frequent evening sessions over a beer on the way home gave Guenther the chance to blow off steam over the frustrations of his job. These frustrations were not only over his daily dealings with his Afghan Police counterparts. At times he was also vexed with the rest of his five-man German Advisory Team. Guenther's team leader hailed from Bremen, which was many miles and a society apart from Guenther's Bavarian upbringing. The team leader was a suave, well-educated man whose personality and demeanor were well-suited to the German Embassy; however, not well-suited to the gritty daily contact with the Afghan counterparts that Guenther experienced.

The third man of the team was a traffic expert. His signature achievement during his five-year tour in Kabul was to have a traffic light erected over the Kabul intersection known as "Blue Mosque Street." This was the first traffic light in Kabul's history. The fact that no one paid any attention to it did not matter to the advisor. At least he had accomplished "something" in those five years. This advisor also had a rough side to him. He obviously harbored bitter feelings over his five-year assignment. When Guenther hosted a farewell gathering at his house, this man was asked if he had any regrets about what he had not done while in Afghanistan. The advisor pulled on his beer (not his first), pondered, and then made his declaration. According to him, he would have adopted a young Afghan boy when he first arrived in Kabul. The advisor would have taught the boy German and English. He would have enrolled him in the International School and then sent him to Germany for further education. Upon the boy's graduation from a German university, the advisor declared, "I would have slit his ---------- Afghan throat." The gasp from the group was audible.

Guenther's tour had been anything but easy, but he had a different outlook. Guenther had enjoyed traveling with Afghan Police throughout the country. Guenther had been embarrassed on several occasions while visiting provincial villages. One of the entertainment traditions for Afghan villagers was listening to traveling storytellers who went from village to village, singing and telling their tales, in return for a meal and a place to sleep. Often, even as late as the 1970s, the subject of their stories was German Field Marshal, Erwin Rommel. Leading up to the Second World War, Germany had been a major source of aid to Afghanistan, both militarily and commercially. Although Afghanistan had remained neutral during the War, they had favored Germany. They had to temper their outward support when their neighbor, the USSR, joined the Allies against Germany. There were a number of German advisors in Afghanistan before and during World War II. From them, Afghans heard stories of the war, but with a German "spin." As natural fighters, the Afghans became intrigued by, and admired, the legend of Rommel. When entering a village, Guenther would be introduced as a German advisor. Guenther would often be greeted with the "Heil Hitler" upraised arm salute by the older Afghan men.

I had advised the former head of our Afghan BNDD Office, Paul Knight, who was now the Regional Director of BNDD in Europe, of Guenther's upcoming departure. Knight arranged for an appropriate gift from BNDD to Guenther. This included a warm letter of thanks from BNDD Director, John Ingersoll. Guenther replied to Director Ingersoll with a letter of his own. He cited the importance of his relationship with Knight and me. Guenther sagely noted to

Director Ingersoll that, "Here we write the year as 1351, and much of our work must be carried out accordingly. As examples: No written, codified statutes, only first names, no birth registry (all dates shown in official documents are estimated and variable), no record of resident aliens, no street names, no house addresses, 93% illiterate, three million nomads, general corruption among officials, an archaic social structure, hopelessly inadequate communication, and more. Under such conditions, good cooperation with officials concerned with the struggle against narcotics traffic becomes a vital necessity."

There was a big hole in our joint enforcement efforts after Guenther's departure.

Chapter 17

THE EMBASSY WAS FORTUNATE TO have a true professional in the person of Richard Schenck, the State Department's Consular Officer for Kabul. Schenck's office was next to mine. I was constantly causing problems for him by having American citizens locked up. When this occurred, he or one of his vice consuls had to go to visit U.S. citizens in jail and see to their needs. This was first at the Firehouse, and then at Dehmazang Prison. He was also the one who dealt with injuries and the deaths of American hippies who came to Kabul.

Schenck never seemed to mind the aggravation, though. He was able to walk the thin line. He provided me with assistance at times, while still maintaining the rights of his "clients." There was a constant stream of hippies coming to his office to report their passport as having been stolen, or other such calamities. Schenck would often know that the passport had probably been sold by its owner, but he always remained polite and non-judgmental. Schenck would give me a heads up if he saw something significant that he thought I should take a look at.

One day in June of 1972, Schenck came in to my office. He said he had received a most interesting visitor in his Consular Section. A man named Ronald Bunzl had come to see him. Bunzl told Schenk that he had heard from "someone" that Schenck was an avid photographer. Bunzl had brought a professional aluminum camera case with him. Nestled in the foam cushioning was a beautiful large format camera base, along with a variety of lenses and attachments. Bunzl was attempting to sell the set. Bunzl had also revealed to Schenck that he had driven from Europe to Kabul in a Ferrari. This was not only unusual, but extraordinary. The roads began to deteriorate once you left Western Europe. They got even worse by the time you had traveled the length of Turkey. After that you were into and across Iran and then through the rugged eastern half of Afghanistan. That was a distance of well over 3,000 miles. Given that he was driving a luxury sports car, Bunzl was very lucky to have made the trip unscathed.

Schenk thought I would be interested in talking to Bunzl. He suggested that I come to his office as a prospective camera buyer. I did so, but avoided giving Bunzl my name or position. The camera was a good buy. We engaged in general chatter, and I told him I marveled at his bringing a Ferrari to Kabul. I asked him why he had done so. Bunzl said he had made contact in Europe with a member of the Afghan royal family. The unnamed Royal told Bunzl that if he purchased a Ferrari and drove it to Kabul, the Royal would pay him back double his purchase price. Bunzl said that upon his arrival in Kabul, the Royal had gone back on his promise. Bunzl was therefore in a quandary. He said he had paid $6,000 for the used Ferrari (a lot of money in those days) and now might be stuck driving it back to Italy. By this time, Schenck and I were exchanging dubious looks behind Bunzl's back. As a test, I told Bunzl that I was not interested in the camera. However, I might be willing to pay him his $6,000 investment and take the car. That would save him the drive back to Italy. He would also save the trip expenses and the effort to sell it there.

As I expected, Bunzl turned down my offer. He said he needed to try to work something out. Bunzl departed the Consular Office and then Schenck and I compared notes. We agreed that Bunzl's story did not add up. Bunzl had arrived at the Embassy in a taxi, not in the Ferrari. I spent that evening cruising by the better hotels, looking to identify where Bunzl was staying. I was trying to locate the Ferrari so that I could get the license tag number. I had no success. A couple of days later I was at the airport looking at freight shipping bills of lading. As usual, I also scanned the recent passenger embarkation and disembarkation cards that all travelers had to prepare. To my surprise, I found that Bunzl had flown out of Kabul the previous day for Europe. The embarkation card provided me with his identifying data, including his passport number. It also identified the hotel he had been staying at; it was not one of those I had checked.

I went to the hotel and told the owner I was looking for an American who had promised to sell me his sports car. The owner informed me that Bunzl had left, as I knew. The car had been picked up by "one of the shipping companies." The owner did not know the name of the company.

I began to search for the correct shipping company with the help of the Embassy's Economic Section officer, Jay Hawley. I learned that the shipping routes to Europe were quite severe and required many different carrier modes. If shipped in the open, a Ferrari would most likely be stolen en route. The car would need to have been shipped in a container. There were four Kabul shipping companies that used containers as a principal method of shipping. One of the companies, The Afghan Transit Company, had been accused of smuggling hashish by European authorities. There was a commonality between the four companies. All of their shipment routes transited the Soviet Union.

The container route from Kabul was by truck through Kandahar, Herat, and Torghundi. The latter town was on the USSR border where the Soviet railroad was located. Non-container bulk shipments were transferred at Torghundi. Containers continued by truck across the USSR border to Kushka. At Kushka, there was suitable equipment to transfer the containers to railroad cars. The USSR route was preferable to shipping via Pakistan due to the inefficiency of the Karachi Port. Also complicating the Karachi route was a lengthy journey; either around Africa to Europe, or via the Suez Canal.

My first stop was to the Afghan Transit Company, whom the European countries suspected of shipping hashish to Europe. I couldn't get in the door there, as one of the mangers recognized me. My luck was better at the Afghan European Transit Company. I told the manager that a friend of mine had recently shipped a car back to Europe. I was considering buying an antique car I had discovered and was exploring shipping alternatives. The manager was very helpful and immediately began shifting through a stack of waybills. He quickly pulled out one with the name, "Ronald Bunzl." The waybill reflected that a Ferrari had been placed in a container and had left only the day before.

Its long journey was from Kabul to Kushka, USSR, and then on to the USSR port of Odessa in the Black Sea. At Odessa the container would be offloaded onto a ship. From there the sea voyage would track one of the world's oldest shipping routes between two continents. The ship would cross the Black Sea and sail past Istanbul, Turkey, on the Bosporus, into the Sea of Marmara, then into the Aegean Sea via the Dardanelle Strait; passing nearby the ancient city of Troy. From the Aegean, it would pass around the boot of Greece, and then continue into the Mediterranean and up the western coast of Italy to Genoa. This was going to be one heck of a journey, costing about the same amount of money that Bunzl said he had paid for the car originally.

I think the manager sensed my excitement. He had seen me write down the airway bill number. I also recorded the license plate number of the vehicle, as well as the container number. It was clear to him that I was there for a different reason than I had stated. He took the waybill and walked over to his copy machine. When he finished there, he handed me a copy. He said, "I think you will find everything you need here." The manger then returned to his desk and thumbed through another pile of bills of lading. Without saying anything, he copied a waybill from the second pile and handed me a copy. Smiling, he said, "You might find this one interesting as well." The second waybill was for a Volkswagen Kombi that had just been shipped. The container that held the VW would cross the Soviet Union by rail to St. Petersburg. There it would be put on a cargo ship. From St. Petersburg it would cross the Baltic Sea, past Denmark, and into the North Sea, to its final destination of Oslo, Norway. The cost of this journey was about twice the value of the vehicle.

My senses told me that I could trust the manger. He looked and acted like a professional. I inquired of his background. I learned that we had a mutual friend in Fred

Seikaly, the owner of Beirut Express, in Lebanon. He was also a friend of Fred's representative in Kabul, Willy Alaily. Armed with that, I properly identified myself to him and told him of my interest in the shipments. I asked him why one would go to such lengths and cost to ship vehicles these distances. The manager explained that Afghan Customs automatically sealed the containers without proper, regulated inspection. If customs suspected there was contraband inside, they just collected a bribe before putting the seal on. When the container reached the Soviet border, Soviet Customs created a new bill of lading. They then added a new seal to the container without checking the contents.

Throughout the journey, new paperwork and seals were added. When the container reached its European destination, it had a sheaf of USSR bills and numerous additional seals. Often, the original Afghan bill of lading had disappeared. European Customs agents did not suspect that anyone would be smuggling contraband out of the USSR. They would usually pass the shipment into their own countries without inspection. I left the shipping company office with the manager's assurance that I was welcome to return to make further inquiries in the future. He would contact me if something caught his attention. I did return several times, and on each instance, with a bottle of good Scotch.

Returning to the Embassy, I sent a message to BNDD Regional Director, Paul Knight, in Paris, and to Frank

Tarallo in Rome. I gave them the details regarding Bunzl's shipment. I did the same for the suspect shipment on its way to Norway. This was June. It took until October for Bunzl's Ferrari to arrive in Genoa, where Italian Customs dismantled the vehicle and discovered 165 pounds of hashish hidden in traps within. On October 25, 1972, Bunzl was arrested when he attempted to take delivery of the vehicle from Italian Customs. On June 14, 1973, Bunzl was convicted of smuggling, sentenced to five years in prison, and assessed a three million lire fine. I was advised in late September of 1972, that the VW was seized in Oslo, also with a load of hashish. Two persons were arrested. These examples of the use of the USSR as a smuggling route to Europe proved important in discussions with Soviet officials over the next year.

Chapter 18

THE SUMMER OF 1972 BROUGHT its usual rush of world travelers to Afghanistan. Generally there were two types of these travelers. The first came looking for adventure and cheap drugs. They would stay a while and then drift further east to places like Goa, New Delhi, and Kashmir. If they were smuggling, it was for their own future use or as a favor to friends back home. The second group was comprised of seasoned smugglers. They worked with others to obtain a regular supply of drugs from reliable sources. They established smuggling systems, arranged for payoffs to officials, and moved the drugs out of Afghanistan by all the various means I have described. The Afghan drug merchants were becoming more and more sophisticated in their dealings with the veteran drug smuggling foreigners.

The dangers for the "world travelers" were increasing. There were increasing reports of robberies and rapes along the long, lonely stretches of Afghan highways. One route was from Herat, near the Iranian border, to Kabul. The Embassy staff learned of the murder of a recently married couple who were from the Philadelphia area. Their bodies had been discovered two hundred yards from the road, where they had parked overnight with their VW Kombi. From evidence gathered at the scene, they had been eating breakfast when they were surprised by two or more men. The couple attempted to flee into the desert, but both were each shot in the back. Further evidence at the scene indicated that they had lived for several hours, lying just a few yards from each other in the hot sun. Impressions in the sand reflected that they had attempted to sit up and drag themselves a few yards towards each other. They had probably been able to speak to each other. They eventually succumbed to loss of blood, dehydration, and shock. Their bodies lay in the desert for several days before being found by Afghan Policemen. Oddly, most of their possessions had not been stolen, but were still intact in the VW. This suggested their assailants may have been frightened off by other road traffic.

Once informed of the murders, the Consular office arranged for the bodies, the VW and the possessions to be transported to Kabul. Upon arrival in Kabul, the remains were taken to the USAID compound. The State Department had notified the parents in the Philadelphia by using identification found in the vehicle. Both were from prominent families. The families were asked to provide possible identifying items because the bodies were in an advanced state of decomposition. The family of the woman described a unique ring that she wore on her right hand. James Murray, a vice consul, who was the only American member of the Consul's staff in Kabul at that moment, asked me to accompany him to the USAID compound to be witness to his attempt to identify the couple. Arriving there, we found that the bodies had been brought to Kabul in long, makeshift cardboard boxes. These had been placed on a wooden stand under a large shade tree in the back of the walled compound. Their VW bus was parked nearby. I suggested that we first search the van for identifying items before examining the bodies. Murray agreed.

There were a number of personal possessions. There were many photographs of a handsome young man and a beautiful young woman. There were photos from their wedding. We found that each had kept a separate journal of their travels from Philadelphia, through Europe and on toward Kabul. We then turned our attention to the remains. I lifted the top pieces of cardboard off the bodies. This was no longer a handsome pair of young newlyweds. Murray and I gasped at the sight of the bodies; burned and blackened by the sun. An army of maggots covered the young woman's chest and the man's torso. Murray, almost in a whisper, asked if I could check for the ring. I wrapped my hand in a rag and then grasped the girl's right wrist to lift the hand free. It was trapped between her body and the side of the cardboard. As I lifted it, her arm separated from the shoulder and hung free in my hand. Murray turned away in obvious distress. The ring, as described, remained on her right ring finger.

It took Murray a bit to compose himself. When he did, he made arrangements for two shipping coffins to be brought to the site. We gathered the possessions, boxed them and took them to the Embassy. I took the journals home with me to read that night. I wanted to learn the purpose of this couple's trip. The journals were fascinating in terms of learning how people can become distant in their relationships; how we can misunderstand another person's thoughts and reactions to events. The lighthearted fun of the adventure of being in Europe, and buying their van, began to wane as they headed east. As they passed through Turkey and into Iran, each wrote of their reactions to the challenges they faced. The challenges included flat tires in the middle of nowhere and running out of food at times due to bad planning. He blamed the low food supply on her bad planning and she blamed his overeating. Oddly, for such travelers, they showed no serious predisposition to drug use. Both had written several negative comments regarding the "wasted" fellow travelers they met along their journey. It was obvious; however, by the time they reached their final stop in the desert and wrote their last journal entries, they were no longer on the same page.

Murray arranged for the shipment of the bodies. He corresponded with the families regarding what effects they wished to have shipped to them. I felt that the last month of journal entries would cause the families great distress, so I recommended that the journals not be returned, and I'm not sure whether they ever were or not. The families could not immediately decide if the VW Kombi should be sold or shipped to the U.S. They suggested that the Embassy make use of it until they had made up their minds. I offered to put it to good use.

For several months thereafter, I used the VW as a surveillance vehicle. It was banged up and battered, so it fit in with its many VW brethren in Kabul. If I was interested in who was frequenting the shop of a known Afghan drug dealer, I could park the vehicle nearby. I would crawl onto the sleeping platform in the back, and from there could observe and photograph activity from behind the VW's curtained windows. The van also served as a prop for another undercover approach I was using. I had acquired a new VW gas tank that some enterprising smuggler had purchased and had converted for his own clandestine purposes. The tank had a sealed partition a short distance past the filler tube. Access to the second half of the tank was via the end plate of the tank. The end plate had been burned off around the connecting edge and replaced with a pre-drilled plate that fit in against a rim. This compartment could be filled with packages of hashish. The end plate was then screwed into the rim and this tank then replaced the original gas tank. The front end of the tank could then be filled with a gallon or two of gas. The underside of the van was then sprayed with a protective sealer substance that was normally intended to prevent rust and corrosion. The vehicle was driven through mud and gunk so that the underside was further coated. The trap at the end of the tank could not be detected without considerable effort.

Once I had enough intelligence from my observations, I would don my "world traveler" garb and engage the suspect storeowner. I would develop a bit of rapport over our common interests. I would then take the owner to the VW, show him the gas tank resting in the back, and explain its application. We would agree that the merchant would fill the empty tank compartment with as much hashish as he could and seal the end. I would tell the merchant that I would return in a few days. Then I would pay him and take the tank to a mechanic who would remove the old gas tank and replace it with the new one. Most of the merchants were delighted with my smuggling ingenuity. I would return a few days later, check the filled tank and, ostensibly, leave to get the money to pay the storeowner for the hashish. I would give the signal, and the police would roll in to make the arrest. I'd retrieve the gas tank for yet another gig.

After successfully using this gimmick several times, I learned that a number of similar tanks had been made by a local welder. Several smugglers were planning to use the technique as well. Their plans were foiled, though. After several merchants had been arrested with my tank, the word spread among the other merchants. Soon, none of them would go near a compartmented tank.

I was still operating on my own in Kabul, aside from my secretary, Delle. She was a great help, as we were receiving an increasing number of alerts for suspect smuggling vehicles bound for Kabul. The Hamburg Police, Frankfurt Police, Royal Canadian Mounted Police, and German Customs had become prolific in their reporting. They all wanted help and follow up on investigations in Kabul. Likewise, BNDD offices along the West Coast of the U.S. were alerting us to suspect vehicles heading our way. I would check for the targeted vehicles on my way to the Embassy each morning. I would ride my motorcycle or drive the Toyota Land Cruiser by hotels that were often frequented by Western smugglers. I would have a list of the suspect license plate numbers that I had been provided. I also enlisted the aid of my sons, Michael 12, and Sean, 10. They took school bus rides across Kabul twice a day. Their route took them past many of the shops of suspect drug suppliers. The traffic in Kabul always just inched along, allowing them to take a good look at the vehicles in front of the shops. I provided each of them with a few plate numbers at a time. They would check the plates of vehicles, looking out of the bus windows for matching numbers. They actually had a few hits over a period of time, which earned them a bonus in their allowances.

There wasn't much I could do about the vehicles in Kabul. I could advise the providers of lookouts with confirmation that their suspects had arrived in Kabul and had visited their drug sources. This information allowed them to try to project when the vehicles would arrive back in Europe or the United States. They could then place their lookouts accordingly.

The summer of 1972 turned out to be a bad spell for the Brotherhood of Love (BEL). Their growth as a criminal organization escalated in Laguna Beach in the late 1960s. BEL members Robert Ackerly, Rick Bevan, Fat Bobby Andrist, Travis Ashbrook, and others, had each traveled to Afghanistan at one time or other. They had established a strong relationship with three Afghan brothers, Amanullah, Hayatullah, and Nazrullah Tokhi in Kandahar. These brothers became the principal source of hashish for the Brotherhood, supplying them with tons of the drug over the years. Amanullah had actually served as a maintenance man in the U.S. Embassy for a number of years before my arrival.

Based on my Afghan investigations that involved the BEL, I was called to the U.S. In Orange County, California, I testified before a grand jury that was investigating the BEL's activities. In August 1972, the BEL Task Force staged the largest drug raid in California's history. The back of the BEL international hashish and LSD manufacturing and distribution operation was broken. Houses and businesses were raided. Almost sixty people were arrested in several states, and the remaining members were on the run. I managed to get the Tokhi brothers arrested in Kandahar, but their incarceration lasted only hours. They had already prepared for that eventuality through their relationship with Kandahar Police. BEL figurehead, Timothy Leary, had been sentenced to ten years in prison in February 1970, but had escaped that September with the aid of the Weather Underground. He and his wife made it to Europe, and then to Algeria where he hooked up with fellow fugitive, Eldridge Cleaver, a leader in the Black Panther movement.

Chapter 19

THE SUMMER OF 1972 WAS also one of enjoying the rugged beauty of Afghanistan. A friend had made his summer house in Paghman available to us. This was located in the mountains just northwest of Kabul. The views were spectacular and the brilliant flowers were amazing. The Afghans who lived in the area were most hospitable. Consul Richard Schenck, his wife Tammy, and their son and daughter would often join us there for a relaxing weekend afternoon and a good meal.

A more adventurous trip was taken with friends from the British Embassy. The British dentist, Jan van der Pant's service to the King and the rest of the Royal family had yielded him a great bonus. Van der Pant had received permission for himself and his friends to visit and camp in the Dari Ajar, also known as the King's Valley. The valley was located about 240 miles northwest of Kabul in the direction of Marzar-e Sharif.

The planning for the trip was finely detailed. We had to carry our gasoline, water, food, clothing, tents and bedding. Our party would include the Burke family, Geoffrey and Irene Cowling, Barbara and Jan van der Pant, and a fourth couple. The Cowlings would also bring one of their local servants.

Plenty of weapons and ammunition were another necessity. Just a few weeks before, three American couples had been enjoying a picnic in the mountains. They were set upon by four Afghan men. One of the Afghans held their single revolver on the three American men while his companions raped the women. They then traded off with the gunmen to give him a turn. We did not intend to let this happen to us.

Our British friends had large Land Rovers, including an extra one driven by their Afghan servant. That vehicle carried most of their gear. The six Burkes had all of their gear strapped to the top and back of our two-door Toyota Land Cruiser. Our children, Michael, Sean, Sheila, and Michele were cramped in the back. They didn't sit on seats, but on a strong plywood platform I had rigged across the seats to allow for storage below. Irene was in the passenger seat with the maps. Off our little caravan went. Our camp the first night was just south of Bamiyan, about 180 miles from Kabul. It had been a tiring trip over rugged dirt roads so far.

Earlier that day I was leading the group. Coming upon a dry stream bed, we were confronted by a large herd of wooly, flat-tailed sheep. I stopped when we reached them. A tall, raggedly dressed sheepherder with a long white beard and turban came running at our vehicle. His face was contorted in anger, and his eyes were black and menacing. He was probably thinking I was going to drive into his herd. He reared back as he reached the driver's door. Lunging forward, he thrust the strong staff he was carrying into my open driver's side window, aiming directly at my head. Luckily, there were no headrests in vehicles in those days as I was able to jerk my head back while striking the pole forward with the flat of my left hand. This diverted the staff towards the inside of the windshield. My police baton rested in two spring clips against the bottom of the flat windshield. I grabbed the baton from its clips with my right hand. I drove the end of the baton with the embedded ball bearing into the throat of the sheep herder. Down he went.

I could now see several other Afghan men running down the hill toward us. I blew the horn and gunned the Toyota forward, splitting the sheep herd. I frantically waved the other vehicles forward, and we got the hell out of there. I figured the sheepherder wouldn't be eating much that night or telling many stories; if he was still alive.

At our small campsite, we drew the vehicles into a rough circle. The five men then fired a volley of rifle and shotgun rounds into the air. That was just to let anyone nearby know that we were armed. The five of us then took turns staying awake throughout the night to ensure that no one tried to surprise us.

The next day took us through Bamiyan where Buddha statues had been carved into the side of the cliff centuries before. The tallest stood 175' and the others a bit shorter. Legend was that they were once covered with gold leaf. The statues were riddled with caves and crevices. Now they were temporary homes to Western hippies who crawled through the structures to the tops for a magnificent view of the valley before them. Years later, the statues would be the hiding place of the Hazarah residents of the valley; first from the Soviet Army and then from the Taliban. In 2001, the Taliban initially attempted to destroy the Buddha statues on the orders of Mullah Mohammed Omar, the spiritual leader of the Taliban. In their first effort they used artillery pieces, but that effort failed. The Taliban then dynamited the statues. That brought them down, but also brought outraged condemnation of their act from around the world.

The following day of our group trip included a stop at the six lakes of Band-e Amir. The lakes were a glimmering blue against the sand colored landscape around them. The lakes were separated by natural dams, with the water falling about 30 feet down from each lake to the next lake below it. The kids delighted in cooling off under the waterfalls.

From Band-e Amir, the road got rougher. At times it consisted only of dry stream beds. Now we were really paying close attention to our maps and compasses. Forty-five miles north of Band-e Amir, walls of red rock began to reach out from the desert. The walls soon began to close in on each side of us. These walls, and the river that ran down its center, were our guide into the Ajar Valley. Beyond the walls, the mountains rose to about 10,500 feet. The walls we followed narrowed before us and eventually merged. There, at the base, was a beautiful lake where the sun rarely shone. Just before that large lake, the river had broadened out into small lake. It was on the grassy banks of the smaller lake that we made our campsite. We were greeted by the King's chief hunter and keeper of the valley, Mir Abdul Shakari. Jan van der Pant showed Shakari our permit from the King. Shakari placed himself and his workers at our disposal.

We had brought a cooler of steaks for our dinners. The kids got up early and caught rainbow trout, which we cooked for breakfast; nobody went hungry. We hiked up to and around the large lake on a narrow stone path that circled the south side. On the far end the walls came together and rose steeply and jaggedly at the head of the lake. It was a truly magnificent place.

One evening, I left the camp with five Afghan men, including the keeper of the valley, Mir Abdul Shakari, and a teenage boy. We climbed throughout the night, reaching an elevation of about 7,500 feet just after dawn. I carried a Danish hunting rifle with a powerful scope I had borrowed from Afghan Police Commandant Askarzoi. Our objective was to hunt the knurly horned Siberian Ibex (mountain goat) that lived in the mountains along with snow leopards. It wasn't long before the teenage boy spotted six Ibex traversing the slope below us at high speed. They were about 200 yards away. The largest of the group was the fifth in line. I realized that picking him off at a dead run would be impossible. I could see that the Ibex were coming up on two huge boulders their path would take them between. I aimed between the boulders about two feet above the ground. I counted off the first four Ibex as they passed through the opening. Then I squeezed and fired. The bullet and the fifth Ibex intersected as he entered the opening. The Ibex tumbled down the mountain, but we were able to recover and dress him before returning to the camp.

That night the kids slept in the tent. Irene and I slept in our sleeping bags outside and under the tent apron. In the morning, Irene said that she had awakened during night and felt that something was roaming around within the camp. I had been exhausted from my previous night's adventure and our friend's celebration of my success. I was so tired that I might not have been awakened, even if someone had driven a tank through the camp. A search of the area proved her correct. We had left the head of the Ibex with its horns out to dry near the small lake, but now it was gone. Searching the area by vehicle, we discovered the culprits about a mile and a half from our camp. They were large, wild dogs, as tall as great Danes and as heavy as Newfoundlands. Somehow, they had carried the large, heavy Ibex head all the way from our camp. A few rounds fired in the air scattered the dog pack. We returned the Ibex head with horns to the camp.

Our companions were able to stay on at the Ajar for several more days. The Burke family had to leave due to my scheduled travel, once again to the United States. Rather than re-tracing our route south, I elected to travel due east. The plan was to hit the north end of the Salang Tunnel and then proceed to Kabul. While it was a rough trip, it took us to a major road more quickly. At one point we hit a hole in a dry stream bed. The Toyota bounced so hard that my son, Sean's, head hit the vehicle's ceiling. Sean left a permanent dent in the roof, and his siblings claimed, also one in his head. We drove through the Salang tunnel and started down the hairpin turns on the south side. That's when it got a bit scary. The hard travel that had preceded the tunnel traverse had heated the brakes to the point that they were ineffective. Going down that long, steep road out of the tunnel was a combination of low gears, the hand brake, and prayers. Not to mention low toned curses, and sweaty palms. From the back of the vehicle I only heard, "Are we there yet?"

When conducting research for this book I discovered an April 2004 article in the Atlantic Monthly Journal. It was written by Jonathan Legard, who is one of the first, if not the first, foreigners to travel to the Ajar since 1979. On Legard's 2004 journey, he spoke with our chief hunter and keeper of the valley, Mir Abdul Shakir, who was now in his mid-sixties. Legard described him as having a snow white beard and watery gray eyes, but still of powerful build. I had captured Shakir's reflection in a 1972 photo taken of him posing with our Ibex. The thirty-two years that had passed since we climbed that mountain together had taken a toll on Shakir. According to Legard, Mir Shakir and his family had been driven from the valley by the Taliban, and had only recently returned to the area. Gone were the deer, the trees were in bad shape, and the trout were few. The trout had been fished with hand grenades by the invaders. According to Mir Shakir, the King's hunting lodge that we had admired on our trip was gone, having been burned to the ground. Now there was not enough water, no home, no animals, and no seed. Mir Shakir and his family were living in a tent. At some point, the government in Kabul had declared the Ajar a national park, but according to Legard's description, it was a park no more.

Chapter 20

KABUL WAS HOME TO AN amazing mixture of personalities, sights and smells. There were the downtrodden Hazaras from the north, who took on the most menial tasks. They could be seen in the streets of Kabul pulling the crudest of carts. These were laden with all types of merchandise, from livestock to machines. Most of the loads appeared to be terribly heavy. At times, they may have had a beast of burden pulling the carts. More often, the Hazaras were the beasts of burden.

There were the carpet merchants, whose shops opened to a wide street with a dusty field beyond it. The merchants would hire very poor Afghan men for mere pennies. These men spent the day dragging newly woven Afghan carpets across the dusty field. The purpose was to "antique" the carpets. This brought a better price from unwary foreigners. They also had a system for the "antiquing" of larger, heavier carpets. The laborers would drag them into the street in front of the shops and let the passing trucks run over them all day.

Then there were the merchants who sold handicrafts, textiles, and pottery to the foreigners. Some of these were legitimate, while some became drug fronts. The latter fed the appetite many of the foreigners had for drugs.

The entertainment industry in Kabul in 1972 was extremely limited. This was mainly due to Muslim laws and edicts. One man who seemed to get around the restrictions was Ali Seraj. Seraj ran one of the only nightclubs in Kabul. Although small and modest by Western standards, the "25 Hour Club" was still a retreat for some. His cliental was quite varied. A number of the foreigners who frequented the club were higher-end drug smugglers and dependents of United States Embassy staff. Other cliental were members of the Royal family. It was also a favorite spot for the U.S. Marine Embassy Guards. Rumors had identified the Marines as one of Seraj's liquor sources. At the senior level in the U.S. Embassy, we knew that sensitive information was being leaked regarding classified Embassy operations, and it appeared that the "25 Hour Club" was playing a part in this issue.

My initial impression was that Seraj might be a supplier to smugglers. After learning more, I began to understand Seraj as more of a "fixer" or "arranger" for almost any type of a deal, as he seemed to have connections everywhere. One of his contacts was a Member of Parliament who was rumored to be operating a morphine base laboratory. Seraj was said to be very adept at linking buyers with sellers.

The tip that Seraj's parliamentarian friend had established a morphine base laboratory was of especially great interest to me. This was a development that we feared, but had expected. I knew that we had to attempt to develop more information. Only then could we judge how dire the problem might be. My plan was to play off Seraj's ego. I wanted to see if, provided the opportunity, he would unwittingly make an introduction for us to his parliamentarian contact. I also believed that an undercover approach might identify the source of the Embassy's classified information leaks.

Toward this end, I convinced BNDD Headquarters to launch "Operation M." I recommended that two U.S.-based agents be sent to Kabul to act in an undercover role. Headquarters agreed to send Miami Agent Harry Heyman and New York Agent Tom Sheehan. Heyman was a big bruising man who could talk you into anything. He was a martial arts expert with whom I had worked closely in Miami. In 1970, Heyman had been the recipient of 44 pounds of near-pure French heroin in an undercover operation against a group of traffickers who controlled much of the East Coast heroin supply. Heyman had taken delivery by himself in a warehouse that was guarded by a number of heavily armed thugs. To maintain his cover, Heyman was "arrested" along with the principal defendants. The eventual cooperation of the defendants resulted in the exposure of major corruption within the New York Police Department. As an indication of Heyman's skill, the main defendant later admitted that when Heyman walked alone into the target's warehouse, the defendant and his armed thugs might have been more afraid of Heyman than he was of them.

Red-headed Sheehan was the strong, silent type. His piercing blue gaze could freeze a man in his tracks. A New York mobster testified at his trial that the only reason he had sold a pound of heroin to Sheehan was because he was afraid of him. The mobster claimed to have seen the devil in Sheehan's eyes.

This pair of agents arrived in Kabul on August 8, 1972. The "script" that I wrote called for them to check into the Intercontinental Hotel. The agents almost immediately became aware that the Pamir Supper Club at the Intercontinental was as much of a watering hole and "nefarious activity center" as I had thought the "25 Hour Club" to be. Perhaps that was because Ali Seraj held court there most evenings before heading off to his own club, and of concern to the agents was the seemingly constant companionship of at least two U.S. Embassy Marine Guards, in addition to a number of Western female companions. Two of the largest hashish smugglers of interest to me, Douglas Felix Carty and his partner, Phillip Moreau, were regular members of this group.

After a few nights in the Intercontinental bar and exposure to Seraj and his entourage, one of the Marines who was constantly with Seraj, invited Sheehan and Heyman to join their group at Seraj's "25 Hour Club." Seraj and his friends had obviously been keeping an eye on these two very large and tough Western visitors. They were unlike anything Kabul had seen since Genghis Khan.

It didn't take long for Heyman and Sheehan to become the hit of Seraj's club. They showed they had money by buying drinks for those who clamored around them. They let it out, by innuendo, that they were mob hit men. They were on the run to "cool off "after a job in New York. The club crew ate it up. Through one of the Marine Embassy Guards, the agents were introduced to club owner, Seraj. Seraj offered up his club manager, Faizul, as a guide and interpreter at their disposal while in Kabul. Faizul was a constant companion over the next days and it became clear to the agents that his job was to determine who they were and why they were in Kabul. It became amusing to the agents to learn that Seraj and his group were suspicious that Heyman and Sheehan were in Afghanistan to assist in initiating a revolution. The agents reassured Faizul that their interests bent toward legal and illegal trade, not over-throwing the government.

Once reassured that the agents were not a threat, Seraj discussed the possibility of a joint restaurant venture in Miami with Heyman. On the illegal side, as expected, Seraj played his main role as an arranger. Through Faizul, he introduced Heyman and Sheehan to a colleague, Jahalel Rahmati, who came across as a significant player in the production of liquid hashish. During the course of their negotiations with Rahmati the agents placed an initial order for approximately 6,000 pounds of liquid hashish to be smuggled from Afghanistan to France in half filled, dark wine bottles. In France, according to Ahmadzai, the bottles would be topped off with wine that would rise to the top, leaving the more dense hash oil to settle at the bottom of the bottle. The bottles would then be labeled as French wine and shipped onward to the United States. The agents had no intention of following through with the deal, as they would have needed to front a very large amount of cash to Rahmati.

When the agents brought up a need for official protection for their illegal trade in Afghanistan, Rahmati assured them that his cousin, the Minister of Interior, controlled the Police and Customs. He also noted that his uncle was a member of the Afghan Parliament. When pressed for evidence of immediate protection, Rahmati said that he paid off the Chief of Kabul Police, the chief of Kabul Customs, and the chief of Kabul Airport Customs.

Rahmati also discussed his use of a trans-USSR smuggling route from Afghanistan to Finland. He bragged of a recent successful shipment of 2,200 pounds of hashish shipped to Portland, Oregon via that route. That had included, according to Rahmati, a payoff to U.S. Customs officers in Portland. The drugs would be shipped in transit through the USSR to Finland and would then be reshipped to the United States as product that had originated in Finland. Rahmati offered Sheehan and Heyman the use of his farm in Gardez Province as a morphine base conversion laboratory.

During the agents' stay, one of the Marine Embassy Security Guards surprised me one morning when he came into my office by warning of two American "gangsters" who were staying at the Intercontinental Hotel. What he failed to report was that one of his Marine buddies had asked to join Heyman and Sheehan's criminal network once he got out of the Marine Corps. In addition, if necessary to demonstrate his sincerity, this Marine buddy offered to "do a hit" for the undercover agents. As their exposure to Seraj increased, several things became obvious to Sheehan and Heyman: Seraj was constantly pumping the Marines and U.S. dependents for information, it was also clear that two of the Marines were supplying Seraj with liquor for his club, and Seraj (and his entourage) were also frequent guests at the Marine Embassy Guard House.

The undercover agents were also introduced at the "25 Hour Club" to a U.S. Army communications specialist who worked at the U.S. Embassy. The specialist soon became comfortable with these two supposed gangsters and freely provided them with details regarding his highly classified unit at the Embassy as well as the clandestine communications work the unit was engaged in. This sensitive information was discussed in the presence of Seraj and his entourage, which included U.S. Marines.

Once Seraj learned of the large amount of hashish and morphine base Heyman and Sheehan were interested in, he steered them away from Faizul and Rahmati, and to a Farhad Gula Ahmadzai. Seraj indicated a personal interest in the smuggling operation for the first time and offered to assist the agents in any way. He cautioned, however, that his name had to be kept out of the operation because he held political aspirations. He did serve as an interpreter for the agents in their initial drug negotiations with Ahmadzai. Ahmadzai impressed upon the agents that he held political power through his tribe, both in Afghanistan and in Pakistan's Northwest Frontier. He claimed to have 50 hashish producing facilities in Paktia Province and the city of Mazir I-Sharif. Ahmadzai described a number of shipping routes he used to move his product to the United States.

Of significance to the purpose of the undercover operation, was Ahmadzai's strong opinion that morphine base was not available at that time in Afghanistan, although he readily acknowledged that morphine base would be a much better product than hashish or opium in terms of movement and profit. He even saw finished heroin as a very attractive potential commodity for Afghanistan to export. What Afghanistan lacked, Ahmadzai declared, were opium conversion chemists.

I had only had a brief meeting with the agents a few nights after their arrival. They had picked me up on a dark street in a borrowed car. Since that meeting, almost two weeks had gone by. Before they left Kabul, I needed to debrief them more fully and securely, which required setting up a secure meeting site. The residence behind ours was occupied by an Embassy communicator whose front entrance faced toward a different street than ours. He agreed to help. After dark, he kept his lights out and the gate unlatched. The lights in my house were turned down. The agents parked a few blocks away and walked to the house. Once inside the compound they circled the house to the back. There the encountered the eight foot wall that separated our two compounds. The Embassy man had placed a box next to the wall; up and over the agents went.

We enjoyed a dinner complete with a decent wine. Then we got down to the debriefing. I learned that Seraj, while having introduced the agents to Ahmadzai and others, had not directly taken the bait. It was not until the agents had made it clear they were looking for morphine base that Seraj had become interested. He and the agents had exchanged contact information and promised to get back in touch.

The agents were glad to be able to unwind for a few hours. My liquor supply suffered for it. Their exit over the back wall was not as graceful as their entrance. They had earned this relaxing evening, though. They had successfully operated in a critically dangerous environment, in one of the more unconventional undercover assignments ever pulled off by BNDD agents. The agents had identified major traffickers, answered our question as to the availability of morphine base, and identified the likely sources of U.S. Embassy security leaks. Ambassador Neumann expressed his appreciation for their work in a classified cable to BNDD Director Ingersoll.

Heyman and Sheehan left Kabul with their cover intact and the ability to return if the situation warranted. Shortly after their departure, I was contacted by a Frenchman by the name of Gerard Lafevre who hung out in Seraj's club. Lafevre asked to meet me, and subsequently he came to my office. He told me about two "mafia" men who had just ended their visit to Kabul. Following their departure, according to Lafevre, Seraj had confided in him. Lafevre said Seraj told him that he would help Lafevre obtain permission to remain in Afghanistan, but only if Lafevre would run a morphine base lab that Seraj would set up. Lafevre further claimed that Seraj maintained that he was in contact with the mafia representatives. These men would return to Kabul in the near future with a morphine base chemist.

Lafevre offered to remain in Kabul in order to help me. He would run the morphine base operation for Seraj and obtain information for BNDD. I was not sure who was "gaming" who, so I declined the offer. I told Lafevre that I knew of the presence of the two men and that I had confirmed they were indeed mafia members. I thanked him for his offer, but I told Lafevre that it was far too dangerous for him to have anything to do with such an operation.

Lafevre was accompanied at our meeting by another frequenter of the club, an attractive young American woman named Jan Horsak who said that Seraj heard I was attempting to hire a secretary. According to Horsak, Seraj wanted her to apply for the job. Through Horsak, Seraj expected that he could learn details about my activities and investigations. That was one offer of secretarial assistance that I turned down.

There was another potential security issue that arose during this investigation. Related to my investigations, distribution of cable traffic between the Embassy and Washington, D.C. was usually limited to the U.S. Ambassador, his Deputy, Sam Lewis, and me. For the safety of the two undercover agents, their presence in Kabul was held extremely close. That was until one night during their stay. Irene and I attended a dinner party at one of the Embassy communication officer's house where a number of people from outside the Embassy were present.

At a point during the meal, the hostess looked down the length of the table and addressed me. "How are your two undercover mafia hit men agents doing here in Kabul?" she asked. There was a sudden silence at the table. I shrugged my shoulders and replied that I had no idea what she was talking about. Her husband appeared to choke on his food. He must have managed to kick his wife's shin under the table, as she winced and changed the topic. The look on his face reflected his awareness that his job was now on the line. He had revealed highly classified information to his wife. While he stayed on in Kabul, I was advised by Ambassador Neumann that "remedial action" had been taken. We were not invited to his house again.

As for the U.S. Marine Embassy Guards and the security-risk U.S. Army communications man . . . I waited a few weeks and then sat down for a chat with their superiors. Their exits from Kabul were quiet, but quick. They never knew what hit them.

In 2010, I was surprised to read a report in the *Huffington Post* on Seraj. The Post reported that, "Prince Abdul Ali Seraj accepted the candidacy for President of Afghanistan only to later abandon his bid in favor of Karzai." In 2011, The Post reported, "Prince Abdul Ali Seraj is a direct descendant of nine generations of Kings of Afghanistan, and also the president of the National Coalition for Dialogue with Tribes of Afghanistan."

In his current online biography, Seraj states that he received his education in Afghanistan and at the University of Connecticut in the U.S. According to the biography, while still in Afghanistan, he emerged as a cross-cultural entrepreneur. He established several successful businesses, including a travel agency, taxi service, advertisement, and employment agencies. In addition had he built several restaurants. After the communist coup d'état in 1978, he escaped from Afghanistan and settled in the United States for 24 years. The biography states that Seraj had a successful career in business development, sales and marketing. According to the biography, he worked very closely with the Reagan Administration to provide whatever was necessary to defeat the Soviet invaders in Afghanistan. After 9/11, when the U.S. planned to attack the Taliban/Al Qaeda, Seraj states that he provided President George Bush an outline of how to proceed in Afghanistan. Finally, Seraj said that he eventually returned to Afghanistan and "continued his charitable work and proceeded to build over three hundred homes, several mosques for the poor in several provinces, and supplied school materials to thousands of students."

"Quite a turnaround," I wrote to Seraj in an email after discovering these revelations. I did not receive a reply.

There were also some very interesting foreigners in Kabul, not all of them hell bent on exploiting the drug trade. There was a Christian family devoted to their conversion mission. They attempted to provide guidance to young "world travelers." They also raised German Shepherds. I bought a pup, thinking it could eventually provide me an element of security as I drove the streets of Kabul at night. "Nomad" grew faster than he could be trained, however. At eight months he was 130 pounds of muscle. The kids would play with him in the yard. They would then race into the house, closing the screen door after them. Nomad would just hurl himself through the screen in pursuit.

I did have some job-related fun with Nomad. The procedure at the airport was to surrender your bag to the ticket agent, who would pass it through a hole in the wall to the Customs agent. The bag would then be examined and placed in a line with others by the steps of the plane. Each passenger would come down the line and indicate which bag was theirs and the bag would be loaded on the plane. As the passengers came out of the terminal, I would have Nomad running along behind the bags, sniffing each one. He had no idea of what he should be sniffing for, as I did not know how to train him. As we went through this charade, the passengers would be staring nervously at Nomad. On a number of occasions, bags would lay unclaimed on the tarmac when the airplane doors closed. They would be taken inside, and low and behold, there would be drugs hidden within them that the Customs agents had missed. No need to train that dog, it was psychological warfare at its best.

There was also someone I viewed as a mystery man. A young New Yorker, Ira Seret, who lived not far from our residence in Shari Nau. I'd spot Seret going in to carpet merchants and handicraft shops. He was usually dressed in a sparkling white shirt and Kalas, the Afghan baggy pants. He often wore the soft wool Afghan beret, the "pakul." Seret was obviously several cuts above the typical civilian Westerners in Kabul. He appeared to be living in Afghanistan fulltime. I had noticed bills of lading for air shipments he had made from the Kabul Airport. I had several shipments checked upon their arrival in New York. They were always clean and held some of the best of Afghan crafts. Even the Customs declarations were correct, which was amazing for a shipment from Afghanistan.

I finally got a chance to meet Seret. Boarding an Ariana Airlines flight in Beirut when heading home to Kabul, I discovered that Seret was my seatmate. He obviously knew who I was. We had a short, awkward time at first. I attempted not to appear to pry regarding what he was up to in Kabul, but I was. We both eventually relaxed and Seret talked about his efforts to establish customers in the U.S. He was developing a market for quality Afghan textiles and art craft. We joked back and forth about what some of the other Westerners in Kabul thought about me.

Later, I'd see Seret about in Kabul and we would exchange a friendly wave. I had decided that he was either the smartest smuggler in Afghanistan or one heck of an entrepreneur. It turned out to be the latter.

In writing this book, I discovered a website for "Seret & Sons" out of Santa Fe, New Mexico. The website described Seret's development as an international businessman. The website stated: "During his 15 years living in Afghanistan, Ira Seret developed a unique style of carpet, fabric, and furniture design. Buying and designing for Anne Klein, Oscar de la Renta, Angelo Donghia, Bloomingdale's, Stark Carpet, and others, Ira Seret and his wife, Sylvia, established themselves as a premier resource to the design community. The Serets began creating and exporting Afghan coats, tents and durries just as Asian style entered the marketplace."

According to the website, in 1979, following the Russian-backed coup in Afghanistan, Ira and Sylvia Seret moved to Santa Fe. There they established Seret and Sons: "a showcase for the extensive private collection they amassed during their time overseas. Seret & Sons quickly became a one-of-a-kind experience and the original store expanded into over 80,000 square feet of showroom and display space. Seret & Sons now houses one of the largest and most unique collections of Asian art." I also learned that Ira and Sylvia developed and run "The Inn of The Five Graces," which has been rated one of the top ten small hotels in the United States.

Two other adventurers arrived in Kabul in the summer of 1972. John and Dave Kunst set off from their home in

Waseca, Minnesota in 1970 to walk around the world. Many pairs of shoes and adventures later, they arrived in Kabul, where they stayed for a number of weeks. They had traversed Iran and entered Afghanistan near Herat. Equipped with their donkey and wooden cart, they had a police escort to accompany them along their way to Kabul. In Kabul, a number of Embassy families and the U.S. Marine Security Guard detachment housed them and fed them.

A former member of the Embassy Consular staff recalled, "It soon became clear that the Kunsts were first-class spongers, absolutely uninterested in the cultures they passed through, and clearly only interested in notoriety and whatever personal gain they might acquire from it. I believe the brothers were "invited" to head on after wearing out their welcome at the U.S. Marine House."

Consular officials warned the Kunsts that they were facing the most dangerous part of their journey. This was the deadly route from Kabul through the Khyber Pass to Pakistan. They were warned that if the two stopped at night, it should be near a police post. The brothers left Kabul in early October. In a few days they had made it about forty miles east toward the Khyber Pass. They stopped their wagon and settled in for the night in a rugged ravine near the road. They had ignored the safety warnings. According to an account given by Dave Kunst, during the night they observed six men robbing the crew of a truck that had broken down near them. John fired a shotgun in the air in an attempt to drive off the bandits. Instead of leaving, the bandits fired their Enfield rifles, striking Dave in the chest and killing John instantly. Dave pretended to be dead while the bandits removed his watch and belt. They then ransacked the wooden wagon. After the bandits left, Dave attempted to flag down passing vehicles. After several failed attempts, a vehicle, carrying either Afghan soldiers or policemen, stopped. The Afghans attempted to halt Dave's bleeding and then transported him to the U.S. Embassy dispensary in Kabul.

The next morning, I received a call from German Police Advisor, Paul Friedrich, who was Guenther's replacement. He advised me of the attack and said he was leaving Kabul to go to the crime scene to assist the Afghan Police in their investigation. At his suggestion, I traveled with him to the site of the shooting. Arrangements were made for transporting John Kunst's body to Kabul. The wagon and their belongings were also brought back and stored at the Embassy. The donkey disappeared.

On December 12, 1972, the Kabul Times newspaper reported that two of the bandits, including the gang leader, Machoo, had been arrested and had confessed to the crime. Four other gang members were still being sought. According to the newspaper, the gang had been routinely robbing vehicle passengers along the Kabul–Jalalabad road.

In the U.S., Dave Kunst took four months to recover from his wound. Then, he and his third brother, Pete, resumed Dave's attempt to possibly become the first circumnavigator of the world on foot. The renewed journey started at the site where John and Dave had been attacked. This time they had a police escort with them to the Pakistan border.

Chapter 21

LATE SUMMER 1972, BROUGHT A mix of frustrations of everyday life in Afghanistan. These included everything from a Westerner trying to deal with his Afghan counterparts to something like a simple traffic accident turning life threatening.

It was also a period of trying to develop significant investigations. The latter were intended to go beyond the borders of Afghanistan and to target the opium and morphine base threat of the future. The investigations did not always turn out as intended, however.

In August I was amused and heartened to learn that I was not the only one frustrated with the Afghan Police. Over a beer at his house, the new German Police Advisor, Paul Friedrich, related that he been helping the police investigate a local robbery. The suspect was a German national. Friedrich had identified a residence used by the suspect and recommended to the police that it be searched. He warned the collaborating police major he was working with that he believed another resident of the house was one Thomas Knorr. He described Knorr as a drug trafficker who had previously been convicted in both Germany and the U.S.

for drug offenses. Friedrich was keen to learn what Knorr might be up to in Kabul. Friedrich arrived at the residence with his six best German trained Afghan Police officers. Friedrich tried, but failed to force the gate. The Afghans retreated under a shade tree while Friedrich circled the large, high walled compound, searching for a possible entry point. Finding none, he returned to the front of the house in time to see a taxicab pull away. Friedrich asked the police major if the man had come from the suspect house, but was assured that he had not.

After several more futile attempts to force the gate, Friedrich again questioned the major about the taxi passenger. The major informed him that the person had come from the house opposite the suspect house, and that this individual had three suspicious looking crates. The major had personally checked the passport of the person and the contents of the crates before letting him leave in a taxi. Yes, the man was Thomas Knorr; the crates contained hashish.

I was not so amused to learn what could happen if a Westerner had a vehicle accident. The general warning was that if you had an accident, avoid stopping if at all possible. You should proceed to the nearest police station, which was true especially outside of Kabul. I was coming back to Kabul from the airport on a dark night in pouring rain. The route from the airport was generally desolate. It was broken by only a few darkened villages on the sides of the hills that paralleled the road. I was traveling about 45 miles per hour, peering out the windshield through the sheets of rain.

Suddenly, ahead of me, crossing from right to left, was a line of donkeys. Each had a split grain sack across him like saddlebags. I was about to learn that those sacks contained manure. Astride the third donkey was a young man. He was frantically whipping the donkeys with a slim stick, urging them to go faster. His efforts did not work. I hit his donkey with my Toyota sedan. The next thing I knew, the young man was sitting on the hood of my car. His donkey had preceded him. After sliding over the car's hood, windshield and roof, the donkey had come to rest on the rear deck of the car. In between was a thick layer of manure that my wipers struggled to remove. I jumped from the car. The young man said he was all right, but his hand was hurting. I remembered the warnings and returned to the driver's seat of the car. Within moments, the car was surrounded by a growing crowd of angry, shouting men. I lowered my driver's window to assess the situation. A man reached through the window and attempted to remove the keys from the ignition. I slammed his arm against the steering wheel with my left hand and pulled my pistol from my belt with my right hand. I yelled, "Back!" in Farsi as I pushed the gun towards his face.

He retreated, but a second figure emerged from the crowd. This man pulled the donkey rider from the hood of the car. He then came to the window and declared, "I am an Afghan Army Colonel, trained at Fort Sill in Oklahoma. I love Americans. When I tell you to, hit the gas and get the hell out of here!" He turned and began shoving men away from the car. "Now!" the Colonel ordered. I immediately executed his command, hurtling through the crowd.

Two days later we had an Embassy "Country Team" meeting. Before we started, Defense Attaché, Colonel Richard McTaggart pulled me aside and informed me that he had heard of my accident from the very same Afghan colonel who had assisted me. The donkey rider was okay, having suffered only a bruised hand. I told McTaggart that I wanted to get a bottle of Scotch to the Colonel to thank him, and I asked if he could arrange to deliver it. "Yes," said McTaggart. "But you had better make it two bottles because you ran over his foot in your escape."

On a later visit to BNDD Headquarters, I discovered the graphic incident report I had completed on the standard government accident form. I learned that it had become a classic for the staff of the vehicle administrative unit. It had been framed and hung on the wall in their office.

My pleas for agent assistance had finally been heard by BNDD Headquarters. Off an Ariana Airlines flight bounced Special Agent Michael Holm. A slight young man with shoulder length curly red hair, Michael exuded confidence, which was interpreted by some as cockiness. Michael had been with BNDD in Seattle since 1969. He was friendly, outgoing, and had a reputation as a good case maker. He specialized in what were referred to as "dangerous drugs," including LSD and the like. Kabul was his first foreign assignment. I welcomed having someone back me up.

Over the next months, Holm did just that, in addition to initiating cases himself. I had developed a very good American informant who had proven to be trustworthy and reliable. John, as I will call him, had developed a relationship with one of our Afghan targets, Ghulam Akbar Khan. Khan had been attempting to set up a morphine base laboratory, but had failed. However, Kahn advised John that he had a contact somewhere outside of Karachi, Pakistan who had an up and running conversion operation. John told Khan of his two American contacts who were looking for a source for a steady supply of morphine base.

Khan agreed to travel to Karachi to meet John's customers (Michael and myself operating undercover). Khan intended to make the trip into Pakistan by bus and then by train to Karachi. Therefore, we had to give him a lengthy lead time, as Michael and I were going to fly there. Once again, the U.S. Consulate staff in Karachi was most helpful. Michael and I checked into the largest, two-room suite in the Karachi Marriott Hotel. I had arranged to borrow a $75,000 flash roll from the Consulate. We would need the flash roll to entice Khan and his contact, who were to bring us a two-kilo sample of the morphine base. My regular Consulate liaison, the young female Vice Consul, offered to bring the money to the hotel. She came in a Consulate car for security reasons. With the help of the Vice Consul, I had contacted the Karachi Police and arranged for them to conduct surveillance and make the arrests. I was a bit worried because we had to share details about Khan's train and physical description.

All was set. I put the money in the bottom of one of my cowboy boots and my pistol in the other, and placed the boots in the bedroom of the suite. The very attractive female Vice Consul wanted to get into the action. She jumped into the big bed in the suite, whipped off her blouse, and pulled the blanket up a ways over her chest. We left the door of the bedroom open. This was to allow the suspect a brief view of what every rich dope peddler was expected to have at his beckoning. Then we waited . . . and waited. Two hours after the appointed time, John knocked at the door. I peered out the security peephole. "Damn!" John was alone. In he came. Frazzled and sweating, he related that he had met Khan's train. Khan was carrying the two kilos of morphine base with him. As they started to walk off the train platform, John and Khan saw that there were police swarming the huge station. Khan panicked and ran back to re-board the train, which was departing for the Afghan border in two hours. Despite John's pleas, Khan refused to once again get off of the train.

I hurriedly called the Pakistan Police officer who was our main contact. We arranged to have John accompany him to the train station in an attempt to locate and identify Khan for the police. We assumed that Khan would have hidden the morphine base on the train somewhere near him. The police would know how to get him to tell them where it was.

The Vice Consul got dressed. She had actually fallen asleep during our long wait. We arranged for the Consulate car to pick her up with the $75,000 and return both to the Consulate. I had already spent $200 of BNDD money on the suite. We still needed a place to spend that night. I had to go to the desk and mumble a reason for exchanging the suite for the cheapest room in the house. John returned, exhausted after racing through the crowded trains with the police in vain. Our Mr. Khan had disappeared, never to be heard from again. The three of us ordered sandwiches and beer from room service. Being the senior man, I pulled rank and got the only bed while Michael and John slept on the floor.

If the Afghans had not yet developed the capability to process opium to morphine base, they were still delivering tons of opium to Iran, where addiction was very high. Some of this was moving on into the Eastern areas of Turkey, which were controlled by the Kurds. The Kurds were some of the most proficient morphine base manufacturers in the world. Their morphine base was still providing the precursor drug for the heroin laboratories feeding Europe, the United Kingdom, and the U.S. I had developed an unwitting informant who thought I was a drug smuggler looking for new markets. I began exploring the potential for him to bring major opium suppliers to us. I needed a reason for them to do so. Thus began our establishment of a "morphine base laboratory." The site was the house a friend let us use for Sunday picnics in the mountains west of Kabul in Paghman. I collected plastic tubs, beakers and any other object I could imagine one might have in a lab. I scoured the small commissaries of the Western Embassies for any ammonia-based cleaning products. Ammonia chloride was one of the essentials in the conversion process. With the cleaning products, at least our lab would smell right.

Then we had to make the bad guys believe we were smart enough to hide our operation from authorities. To this end we created a false wall between our lab and its front, a photo developing lab. Again, we were scrounging equipment from Embassy supply rooms and the bazaar; anything that looked like it might belong in a 1970s era photo lab. I had found some large, five-gallon green glass chemical containers. They nestled in straw filled crates. Needing a smelly liquid in them, I emptied a couple of cases of Pilsner Urquell beer. We also needed more manpower. Michael Holm looked too young and too much like a hippy to be a big time morphine base operator. My face was becoming too well known in Kabul, so I called for the cavalry.

Agents Al McLain and George Miller arrived from Beirut, Lebanon and Mike Hurley from Ankara, Turkey. Hurley brought the large flash roll. A cooperating Embassy official in Beirut allowed McLain and Miller to send weapons ahead of them to Kabul in the diplomatic pouch. The time had come to inform the Afghan Police of what we were up to. It was not long after my doing so; however, that the investigation began going south. Hurley, Miller and the informant met with the opium traffickers and showed them the "laboratory" and our photo lab operating as a front. Afghan Police detectives, Holm, McLain, and I provided back up security. The deal was for six tons of opium. When the trucks carrying the opium arrived at our site, we would slam the compound gate closed behind them.

Then a hang up in the negotiations soon reared its ugly head. In typical opium smuggler fashion, the Afghans demanded a hostage. They would hold the hostage until the deal had gone down safely. Bravely, but not wisely, Holm volunteered to be the hostage. Colleagues who dealt with Holm later in his career, jokingly suggested that I should have given him up as a hostage. That was not to be I decided.

Complicating this part of the negotiation was that a couple of the Afghan policemen kept popping their heads above the garden wall. They wanted to see what was going on. Hurley and Miller saw them and believed that the suspects may have as well.

The initial undercover negotiations had seemed to have gone well. We had hopes the full operation would go through. The traffickers claimed to have six tons of opium within several days travel from Paghman. Whether it was our refusal to offer a hostage that tipped the deal, we didn't know. Neither were we sure if the policemen on the wall had spooked them, or if they had been tipped off; we would never know. However, our Afghan informant suddenly broke contact with us and disappeared. We learned that the Afghans Hurley and Miller negotiated with had checked out of their Kabul hotel in a hurry and also disappeared.

We waited a couple of days, but had no further contact with the informant or the suspects. We broke down the operation and returned the borrowed equipment. After Thanksgiving dinner at our house, the agents headed home. "Coincidentally", a week later, the Iranian border police stopped four Afghan trucks. They were coming from the direction of where our suspects said their opium was. The Iranians seized six tons of opium from the four trucks.

Chapter 22

SHORTLY BEFORE CHRISTMAS, 1972, U.S. Ambassador Neumann called a small number of the Embassy staff to his office. This included his Deputy, Sam Lewis, Sam Rickard, the Administration Section Chief, Jim Kelly, Defense Attaché Colonel McTaggart, and me. The Ambassador had just returned from a meeting with Afghan Prime Minister Mousa Shafiq and the German Ambassador. Shafiq had informed the Ambassadors that he had intelligence and proof that The Palestinian terrorist group, the Black September, had sent a six-man team into Afghanistan. This was the same terrorist organization that had kidnapped and murdered 11 Israeli athletes and staff and a German policeman at the summer Olympics in Munich. Their mission was to kidnap or kill Ambassador Neumann and the German Ambassador.

Ambassador Neumann had just finished sending an "Eyes Only, Immediate" cable to Washington, D.C. describing the threat. Now he was seeking the advice of his senior staff. These were officers who might become immediately involved in the protection of the Embassy and the Ambassador. I looked around the room and thought that he could not have a better team to assist him. Each of those present had extensive experience in responding to extraordinary circumstances. The group immediately set about looking at options. Obviously, the security on the exterior had to be increased. The current configuration of two Afghan police at the open gate, each with a six shot revolver, would not cut it. That fact must not have escaped Prime Minister Shafiq. Almost as we spoke, Afghan Police reinforcements began arriving at the gate.

The interior of the U.S. Embassy had obviously not been designed from a threat perspective. A walk up the outside steps brought you through large glass doors into an open lobby. A lone Afghan receptionist sat at a desk about 20 feet from the door. Behind him rose a wide, open staircase with one landing that led to the Ambassador's suite, and the Political and Administrative Sections. To each side of the entrance ran a short corridor. On the west side, or to the visitor's left, was the Consular Office, then the BNDD Office. There was a corner and then a hallway that ran north to the Economic Section. To the visitor's right was a similar corridor and a similar office configuration. Not a great set up in the event of an emergency.

Sam Rickard was the first to leave the meeting. Destined, I was sure, to check with his exceptional contacts in the Afghan Government and foreign embassy community. He would want to gather what additional information he could. Rickard would also be calling his German Embassy counterpart to coordinate their responses. Defense Attaché McTaggart was next, leaving to reach out to his equally good Afghan military contacts. McTaggart would have also been checking to determine what U.S. military assets would be available, should they be needed. McTaggart was a third generation U.S. Army professional. His grandfather served during the Civil War, and his father served in Cuba during the Spanish–American War. Managing adversity was in his bloodline.

As the Embassy Administrative Officer, Jim Kelly was responsible for the small Marine Embassy Security Detachment. He would be coordinating their response with the Non-Commissioned Officer in Command (NCOIC). It was Kelly who bore the greatest burden. The tragedy that occurred during the 1972 Munich Olympics was fresh in everyone's mind. Kelly knew that the Embassy lacked the most elementary security standards for such a dire threat. His first action was to contact the State Department and request immediate assistance. The Department's anemic response was to send one security officer from Beirut. (And who says September 11, 2012, Benghazi, Libya was an anomaly for the State Department?)

Kelly had his local staff start building ¾ inch, floor to ceiling plywood barricades at each far end of the corridors leading off the lobby. At my request, they built a hinged, one-foot square door at eye level just outside my office. I instructed the by now very frightened receptionist that if terrorists gained entrance to the lobby, he should immediately drop under his desk. From there he should activate the panic alarm that had just been installed. I told him that either Agent Holm or I would immediately thereafter be dropping the small door. We would level anything in the lobby with shotgun blasts. That must have been very comforting to the receptionist.

The State Department's immediate answer to the threat was almost as bad as the threat's bite. Arriving on the next flight from Beirut was a short, rotund, security officer. The next morning he joined the "Country Team" meeting. By this time, the entire Embassy's American staff knew of the threat. Ambassador Neumann introduced the security officer, thanked him for coming, and asked him to describe his security plan. In a bellicose manner, the security officer announced that he was aware the Ambassador intended to carry out his full schedule of Christmastime, holiday affairs. These would be held at the Ambassador's residence and at various Western Embassies. The security officer announced that he would be armed and at the Ambassador's side at each of these functions. The officer then described certain hypothetical physical characteristics of an individual. Should such a person approach the Ambassador, the security officer would put a bullet between the person's eyes. Several of those at the table gasped. I leaned over to the

Deputy Chief Sam Lewis, and whispered in his ear, "He just described the Prime Minister."

That afternoon, the security officer took several of the local Afghan security staff to an area behind the Embassy. He had already used the Embassy repair shop to have the barrels of a couple of shotguns sawn off short. After their target practice, he returned to the Embassy. He then began bragging to anyone who would listen, how the locals had suffered gashes in their foreheads from the sawed off barrels. They had not followed his instructions on how to hold the weapon securely in firing, he declared.

Up to this point, my protection and security role had been limited to making a few suggestions to Administrative Chief Kelly. That mode ended abruptly the next morning when I was called to the Ambassador's office. Ambassador Neumann informed me that, upon the Ambassador's order, the State Department's security officer was boarding a flight back to Beirut, Lebanon. Ambassador Neumann said from that point forward, he was entrusting his personal safety to me.

The German Government's response to the threat was in stark contrast to that of the U.S. State Department. There was suddenly present in Kabul a detachment of the Grenzschutzgruppe 9 der Bundespolizei, Border Protection Group 9 (CSG9). This Group had been founded just that summer as an anti-terrorist unit. The group was the German

Government's response to the 1972 Munich Olympics tragedy. While only a new unit, the members had been drawn
from the best of German forces. Sam Rickard and I met with
the group's leader at the German Embassy to coordinate
our response to the threat.

Although we were in a non-Christian country, it
was Christmastime. Ambassador Neumann held and
attended several social, holiday events. I was always
nearby, attempting to blend into the woodwork. Mike
Holm would prowl the perimeters ready to alert me to
anything suspicious. The culmination of the season for
the Christian community was always the Christmas Eve
Mass, which was held at the small chapel located on the
grounds of the Italian Embassy. Ambassador Neumann
and the German Ambassador had been invited as special
guests and declared their intention to attend, no matter
the threat. The Afghan Prime Minister had reported that
morning that the Black September group had been tracked
to Kabul, but the group's whereabouts had not been pin-
pointed. The tension could not have been higher.

I arrived at the Ambassador's residence well ahead of
his departure time for the chapel. I arranged to have two
steel plates with cushions placed over them on the rear
floor of the Ambassador's large sedan. When Ambassador
Neumann entered the vehicle, I requested that he lay across
the cushions. I placed myself with one knee on the back

seat and left leg over, but not on the Ambassador. This allowed me to cover him partially, but to still see out and cover the windows. An armed Embassy military staffer was in the front passenger's seat. The Ambassador did not complain. He had survived Dachau and Buchenwald; he was not going to mind this discomfort. The Italian Embassy was surrounded by Afghan and German Forces. Mike Holm, well-armed, remained on the outside of the chapel with most of the German GSG9 personnel. I entered with the Ambassador. The head of the GSG9 unit was there with the German Ambassador. I was wearing a pigskin leather trench coat. I had cut out the coat's pockets years before to facilitate drawing my pistol in cold weather. This time I carried a UZI, courtesy of my new German colleague. It was slung from my shoulder, under my coat. I knew that he had the same armament under his coat.

These precautions had appeared fine in our planning session. But now, with everyone present in the chapel, I wasn't so sure. The chapel was so crowded that we would have been challenged to have been able to bring our weapons to bear. Very few of the people there knew of the drama that was playing out. The room quickly became almost insufferably warm. Most others removed their coats. My German counterpart and I stood there with sweat running down our faces and backs. I saw Irene glance back at me with concern on her face. The German, U.S. and British

Ambassadors individually had to read a portion of the mass. My German colleague and I exchanged glances. We had shared the thought that this would be a most opportune time for The Black September to make their statement.

Finally, the Mass was over. The second best time for the Black September to attack would have been as the motorcade left the Italian Embassy compound on to the main road. Ambassador Neumann had taken his place on the floor. I was over him, covering one side of the vehicle and Mike Holm knelt on the rear seat prepared to fire out the other side. The motorcade made it back to the Ambassador's residence without incident. Merry Christmas!

What came next was very surprising and very suspicious to me. Within a day or two after Christmas, Prime Minister Shafiq met with the two Ambassadors. According to his intelligence service, The Black September group had been stymied by the "Afghan security response" to the threat. They had abandoned their mission and left the country. This explanation, and Sam Rickard not having been able to confirm the original information, caused me to wonder whether the threat had ever really existed. Had this been some move by Prime Minister Shafiq to curry favor with the U.S. and German Governments by successfully "foiling a terrorist plot?" Ambassador Neumann was gracious in his thanks to BNDD Director John Ingersoll for the support BNDD had provided him during this crisis.

Prime Minister Shafiq was ousted in the 1973 coup against King Zahir, but he survived temporarily. He was arrested in 1978 in the coup let by the Afghan Communist Party. Shafiq was executed in 1979.

Chapter 23

DECEMBER 1972 WAS ALSO A busy month for other reasons. The media had suddenly become aware of Afghanistan and the drug trade. Top journalists such as Bernie Weinraub and Henry Kamm, both from the New York Times, and Robert Kaylor of UPI, came to Kabul on a regular basis. Bill Drummond of the Los Angeles Times and Leon Daniel of UPI came, looked, and wrote their stories. Each of them was more than happy to share a meal at the Burke's home, not to mention a bit of Chivas Regal in front of the fire. They were real professionals and I enjoyed their company.

The USAID folks had bristled when I suggested that their aid to farmers in the Helmand Valley was making it easier for the farmers there to grow opium. After an evening at my house, Bernie Weinraub decided to find out for himself. Weinraub had gone from a copyboy at the New York Times to bureau chief in New Delhi. In between, he had taken assignments in London and Saigon. Now he was driving down a dusty road in the Helmand Valley many miles south of Kabul. He was able to photograph an Afghan farmer tilling his fertile opium field with a tractor that had the familiar USAID handshake on its hood. The irrigation for the field was provided from a USAID water project. That photo and Weinraub's accompanying story made the front page of the New York Times a week later. I denied being part of a conspiracy when the article was relayed to the Embassy from The State Department.

Henry Kamm was one of the New York Time's most prolific international journalists. In late December 1972, he wrote of a girl he called Melanie. Melanie had died on November 5, 1972. She had smoked 26 pipes of powerful opium in the New Istalif Hotel in Kabul. Kamm obtained Melanie's journal, which told of an idyllic journey from Emerson College in Boston to Kabul. Her written description of her trip was in stark contrast to the squalid room where she died. Kamm quoted from the journal as he tracked Melanie's trip from reality. I believe the article won a Pulitzer Prize for Kamm.

Shortly after Melanie's death, Mike Holm made an undercover buy at the New Istalif Hotel. The deal was for 20 pounds of opium and 30 pounds of hashish. The seller was Abdul Wahid, the manager of the hotel. He had sold Melanie the opium that had killed her. When the Afghan Police moved in for the arrest, Holm told Wahid that he was a murderer. Wahid denied it and told Holm, "Your people are killing themselves." We asked the police to throw away the cell door key.

Mike Holm then conducted undercover negotiations for 220 pounds of high grade opium from an Afghan Army Captain. The Captain delivered 50 pounds at his government apartment where he was arrested. William Drummond of the Los Angeles Times was at my side when we entered the apartment with the police. Drummond filed his report on the raid and the other enforcement actions we had been taking. It was a major story for the L.A. Times. It was helpful for us to draw attention in Washington, D.C. as to what we were up against. Drummond went on to be an award winning national writer on the Civil Rights Movement and is currently a professor of journalism at Berkeley.

Late December brought my first break in doing something about the use of shipping containers for smuggling drugs. I had shown that containers were leaving Afghanistan and transiting the Soviet Union to Europe with impunity. I had no formal way of contacting the Soviets in order to share my information. So I got in my Land Cruiser and drove across Kabul to the massive Soviet Embassy. I did not have diplomatic plates on my vehicle and that made for a long wait at the Embassy gate. In contrast to the U.S. Embassy, the Soviets had Soviet military guards at their gate; not like our ragtag Afghan lot. Once inside, my U.S. diplomatic passport came into play and provided me with a bit of credibility. The receptionist called somewhere in the building. She presumably relayed my request to speak to "someone" regarding a smuggling problem. I was actually laughing to myself because right then they were probably racing around, possibly thinking they might have a U.S. Embassy defector on their hands. I could imagine them calling the airport to have the ever present USSR aircraft on standby to hurry me to Moscow.

Instead of being flown off to Moscow, I met with one of their officers. Eugene Chapligin, who was a well-built man, possibly in his early forties. He spoke excellent English and proved to be very suave and well educated. I was very straight forward as to the reason for my visit. I told Chapligin that I wanted to share information regarding the use of the Soviet Union as a smuggling route to Europe. Chapligin seemed startled at the proposal, but genuinely interested. I told him that I would be able to document my assertions. I gave him a report that described the shipping methods being used to move drugs through the USSR. I provided him with information on Ronald Bunzl, including an Italian newspaper clipping of his arrest in Milan. The clipping told how Bunzl had been arrested after shipping his hashish laden Ferrari from Kabul through the USSR.

Chapligin thanked me. He said he would consult with his superiors and contact me in the near future. I left the Soviet Embassy, certain I could hear camera lenses clicking from behind every pillar. I returned to our Embassy and reported the meeting to the Ambassador. He had been the only one who knew of my plans in advance. He was most pleased with the results. Ambassador Neumann was a political appointee, not a career State Department official. He knew that my stepping on State Department turf might well draw anguished howls from his State officers. He was looking forward to pulling their musty coat tails. I told him of my thoughts regarding the Soviet plane at the airport. That drew a hearty laugh. He suggested I was damn lucky they had not shipped me off to Moscow, whether I had volunteered to go or not.

Ambassador Neumann then called Sam Rickard to his office. The Ambassador had me tell Rickard of my meeting with Chapligin. I thought Rickard was going to have a heart attack. His throat became red and his face darkened. "The Soviet Embassy was the Political Section's purview," he declared, "BNDD had no call to be developing contacts there." The Ambassador seemed to be enjoying Rickard's discomfort. He asked if Rickard had not recently lamented that his office had not been able to develop any contacts within the Soviet Embassy. Rickard admitted that he had. "Well, now we have one," countered the Ambassador. I told Rickard that I would be happy to share any information I developed. I would provide profiles on anyone I met, and I would be on the lookout for anything that could help him.

This seemed to mollify Rickard. Not to mention that he was not about to challenge Ambassador Neumann. I had made a copy of Chapligin's business card and gave the copy to Rickard. He said he would run a trace on Chapligin and get back to me. I'm sure the same type of tracing was taking place on the card I had left at the Soviet Embassy. That was my one worry. I had never been named in any of the exposes of CIA officers during my time at the Agency from 1960 through 1970. However, while in Thailand and Laos from 1961–1963, I was declared as CIA to the Thai Government. That was necessary as I was in Thailand under the cover of a civilian advisor to the Thai Border Police. We knew that the Soviets had thoroughly penetrated the Thai Foreign Ministry. It was likely the Soviets had me on record. My hope was they would not conclude that my approach might be some sort of a provocation.

Rickard asked me to come to his office the next day. He said that Chapligin was a member of the Soviet GRU, their largest intelligence agency. His mission appeared to be the recruitment of personnel from various foreign embassies in Kabul. He was considered very intelligent and clever. Several days later, their checks probably completed, I received a call from Chapligin. He invited me to his residence for a drink after working hours, and I accepted.

Meeting with Chapligin in his home was interesting. He was the only member of the large Soviet Mission who lived outside the Embassy compound. This probably spoke to his responsibility to mingle with other foreign diplomats.

I was very aware that our conversations were probably recorded. The several meetings we had were relaxed, however. I learned that the stories of a Russian's ability to enjoy quantities of vodka were not exaggerated. An important issue for us was how to establish tactical communications. I needed to be able to quickly pass information on suspect loads going through the USSR. We also discussed the need to push our dialogue to a higher political level. The objective was to cause action to be taken in the USSR. Towards that end, we agreed on talking points to be passed by our respective Embassies to Washington, D.C. and Moscow. Chapligin wanted to be sure Soviet Customs acted on the information and advised him of the results.

I drafted cables to both Washington, D.C. and the U.S. Embassy in Moscow. The messages provided details of the smuggling systems and of the meetings with Chapligin. I cleared the messages with the Embassy Political Section and DCM, Sam Lewis. We soon had our first response. On February 2, 1973, the Moscow Embassy Economic Counselor and the Embassy Science Attaché, Jack Tech, met with E.G. Nanov from the Soviet Ministry of Foreign Affairs and with the Deputy Chief of Main USSR Customs. The meeting was very productive. Nanov agreed to provide any information that they developed. In turn, they asked for the U.S. to identify couriers, routes and modus operandi. They also requested to receive alerts on suspect shipments.

The Soviets said they had been aware of some shipments of drugs from Afghanistan to Finland. The drugs had been concealed in consignments of equipment.

My contact with Chapligin continued over the next months until that joking reference to a trip to Moscow became a reality.

Chapter 24

MEANWHILE, ENFORCEMENT ACTION WAS PICKING up. The Afghan Ministry of Justice had assigned two civilian Afghan investigators, Mangal and Hazizullah, to be our contacts with Afghan authorities. We decided to conduct a test case with them. I negotiated for 22 pounds of opium and 88 pounds of hashish from a Mohammed Kassim. I had worked undercover against his partner, Abdul Ahad just a month earlier. Ahad had been arrested, but Kassim had evaded arrest at that time. The police considered Kassim a dangerous criminal. He and several others had escaped arrest at the house he and Ahad had shared. They had run through compounds that adjoined Ahad's house. Kassim and Ahad had apparently not communicated regarding who had been behind Ahad's arrest. Kassim bragged to me that he had just sold 225 pounds of hashish to an American. That person had concealed the drugs in his VW van for shipment to America.

I met with Investigator Mangal after obtaining drug samples from Kassim. I had arranged to meet Kassim later. Mangal advised that he would need thirty men to surround the huge compound complex. Mangal further said that he believed Kassim would not supply the drugs, but instead, he would attempt to rob me. With that warning in mind, I met Kassim and another man that evening. This meeting was purposely away from Kassim's house for safety reasons.

I put off the delivery of the drugs until the next day by telling Kassim I would not have money until then. The attempted delivery the next day at Kassim's compound turned into a huge debacle. I had been guided there by an unidentified suspect in my car. As we approached the compound, the large police presence became noticeable. I was able to keep the suspect distracted, but it was too late for Kassim. He had spotted the police and attempted to flee. Investigator Mangal saw him running and had taken him into custody. This occurred outside of the second suspect's view. That suspect began wandering around the compound looking for Kassim. He told me to wait while he checked the rear gate. A moment later a young boy came from the side of the house. He ran back when he saw a policeman peering over the compound wall. I feared that a warning was about to be given. I went to the front gate where a third Afghan was looking out. He turned out to be Kassim's brother, Sher Mohammed. I asked him where the drugs were, and he told me to come with him into the house.

At that moment, the back gate, which could be seen through the courtyard, opened. The young boy entered and yelled to Mohammed that the police were there. Mohammed told me to escape immediately. I tried to calm him, but the others had already started to flee. I gave the arrest signal to Agent Mike Holm, who had been waiting outside the compound. The police team arrested Mohammed, but the boy and second suspect escaped. A search of the compound yielded two tin trunks containing 211 pounds of hashish. Packing material and pressing equipment was also discovered. Kassim and his brother had both been armed.

A few days later a series of events occurred that could not have been more unexpected or bizarre. On Sunday, January 14, I was enjoying a beautiful winter day with my family at the small ski run just outside of Kabul. Late in the morning, I looked up to see Ariana Airlines flight FG 710 pass overhead. The Boeing 727 aircraft was en route to Kabul from Beirut, Lebanon. Aboard that aircraft a businessman had recognized one of his fellow passengers as U.S. fugitive Timothy Leary. The businessman later reported that he had become angry when he realized who Leary was. The man's business partner's teenage son had been attending boarding school in Switzerland a few years before. The boy had become entranced with Leary's mantra, "Turn on, tune in, drop out." Leary had written those words to describe the psychedelic experience. He also used the phrase to promote the use of LSD among young people. The young boy had adopted the concept. He had become a user of LSD. During one "trip" he had climbed to the roof of one of the Swiss school's buildings. He had tried to fly like a bird, but instead of soaring as Leary had promised, he fell to a tragic death.

It was time for revenge. The passenger notified the American flight crew that Leary was aboard. He advised them that Leary was a fugitive wanted by U.S. authorities. The captain radioed Charles Bennett, Chief Ariana pilot in Kabul, with the news. In turn, the Bennett contacted the U.S. Embassy duty officer, James Senner. Senner and fellow Consular Officer, Jim Murray, rushed to the airport. There they explained the situation to the airport security director, Samad Azhar. Leary deplaned in the company of three other persons. They were Joanna Harcourt, Richard Viertel, and Don R. Bell. Also traveling with Leary was his friend and BEL colleague, Dennis Martino. No one at the airport realized Martino was a member of Leary's entourage, and he managed to slip out of the airport unnoticed.

Senner identified Leary to Azhar. Timothy Leary, with bright blue hair, presented a U.S. passport K2581808, which was promptly confiscated by Murray because it had been previously revoked by the U.S. Department of State.

In the airport arrival room hung a sign. In several languages, the sign declared that every traveler was required to have the equivalent of $200. This had to be in some legitimate currency. Anything less and you could not enter the country. Leary and his friends did not have $200, even between them. An Afghan officer informed the trio that without sufficient funds they could not enter Afghanistan legally. They were to be taken into custody until their fate could be determined. The three were then transported to the Plaza Hotel. Timothy Leary and his companion, Joanna Harcourt, were placed in one decrepit room and Viertel in another. Guards were placed outside their doors. Leary had expected they would be staying at the Intercontinental Hotel when they arrived in Kabul. The Plaza was no Intercontinental by any stretch.

Various articles in magazines and books state that I spotted Timothy Leary in Kabul and had him arrested. I actually knew nothing of the activity surrounding Leary's detention until I returned from skiing with my family that afternoon. Jim Senner called me and advised me of the day's events. I had, of course, heard of Leary and of his escape to Algeria. There he had joined Black Panther fugitive, Eldridge Cleaver. Beyond that, I knew no details of his escape. At that time I did not even know much about his relationship with the Brotherhood of Eternal Love (BEL).

The following day, Police Commandant Hakkim contacted the Embassy. He advised that the Afghan Government intended to deport Leary from Afghanistan. The basis for the deportation was that he had entered Afghanistan without proper documentation or sufficient funds. Hakkim's action was actually the result of Ambassador' Neumann's request to Prime Minister Shafiq. At the Embassy we began to initiate arrangements for getting Leary back to the U.S. The next departing Ariana Airlines flight was to be on January 17, which was two days away. The route was to be: Kabul, Tehran, Istanbul, and Paris. There we would have to pick up a flight to London; then the Pan Am polar flight direct to Los Angeles.

Over the next day, we had a lot of activity. I received authority from BNDD Headquarters to expend funds to pay for my travel and Leary's to Los Angeles. I had learned of the poor health of Joanna Harcourt and her refusal to be separated from Leary. I convinced BNDD that paying her way back as well would result in less resistance from Leary. I also convinced them that we should fly first class once we changed from Ariana Airlines (which had no first class) to Pan Am in Paris. I argued that I didn't want a bunch of hippie backpackers jumping me in economy in an attempt to rescue Leary. Luckily, BNDD Foreign Desk officer, Jerry Moers, agreed. Moers did a great job getting me the support I needed to make the rendition work. That was not the first time I had received his support, and it wouldn't be the last time.

"Immediate" precedence cables were flying back and forth among the embassies in whose countries we would pass en route to the U.S. It was necessary to carefully coordinate the travel. We had to ensure that the pair would not be allowed to enter the countries we would be landing in. Finally, on January 17, 1972, Leary and Harcourt were delivered to the Kabul Airport by a contingent of Afghan police. I was waiting at the door of Ariana Airlines Flight FG 70. Agent Michael Holm waited at the bottom of the steps. He liked to refer to himself as "Johnny Justice." As Leary and Harcourt reached him I heard him say, "Holms the name; dopes my game." I cringed. I really cringed later when I read that Harcourt had erroneously attributed that dumb phrase to me.

I introduced myself to the pair and guided them to their first row seats. My seat was just behind them. I told Leary he must realize that the time for running was over. Afghanistan was not a pleasant place to be incarcerated. That was especially true given his obviously ill companion (Harcourt was very jaundiced). Both of them showed the rigors of the past few days. I joked with Leary. I told him that most defendants in the U.S. were bonded out of jail before I had completed the paperwork documenting their arrest. I did not mention that I knew bond had been set at $5 million.

In the 2006 biography "Timothy Leary" by Robert Greenleaf, the author describes a sometimes fictional account of the detention of Leary and his return to the U.S.. There was no world press in Kabul documenting their detention. Harcourt did not perform a "Scarlett O'Hara act for the Afghan Police. There was no woman police officer at the airport or anywhere else in Afghanistan at that time. Michael Holm said "Holm's my name, dope's, my game." I did not return Leary's passport to him. There was no other law enforcement presence on the flight from Kabul other than myself. I was not armed. No "two blue suited agents with 357 magnums" were on the plane. The flight was not diverted from Orly Airport because the airport was closed for the night. In Frankfurt, we were not sur-rounded by armed agents. A German Customs agent and I had Harcourt examined by a doctor at the airport clinic. Harcourt did not have to scream for a doctor, as Greenleaf described. There was no fuss or loud behavior from anyone. Leary did not scream while we were at Heathrow Airport in London. Leary was not on a "blacklist" in England for hav-ing smoked marijuana with John Lennon and Yoko. There was no curtained special section for them on the Pan Am flight to Los Angeles. There was no Pan Am stationary for Leary to write notes on. Leary was arrested on the plane on arrival in LA., He and Harcourt did not walk off the plane "hand in hand." He was wearing handcuffs by that time. I wish that all authors would contact eye witnesses to a story before they write it.

During the first leg of the flight to Tehran, I did my best to put the two of them at ease. If they got some much needed rest, I believed, I would have a better chance of getting their cooperation. Tehran was a fueling stop only and per routine, no passengers were allowed on or off the plane. The next stop, Istanbul, proved to be very "interesting." We drew to a halt on the tarmac some distance from the terminal. The plane was quickly surrounded by military tanks and armored vehicles and a number of Turkish military and police came aboard. The commander announced that, for "security" reasons, no passenger was going to be allowed to disembark. This made the Istanbul-bound passengers very unhappy. Accompanying the Turkish authorities was BNDD agent Art Egbert who was assigned to the Istanbul BNDD office. Egbert advised me that upon our arrival in Paris we would be met by BNDD Regional Director Paul Knight. Knight had arranged for us to be remanded in an international area of the terminal. There we would wait for the morning flight to London and then on to Los Angeles.

As we flew from Istanbul in the dark, our plans for a structured overnight in Paris evaporated. The steward came to me and asked me to come to the flight deck. There, the captain informed me that we were not going to Paris; instead we were going to land in Frankfurt. All passengers would be dropped off in Frankfurt. The wife of the Afghan Ambassador to Italy had died in Rome so the plane was to go from Frankfurt to Rome without passengers. In Rome they would pick up the body of this woman and return it to Kabul. I returned to my seat and began to try to figure out how I would handle a midnight arrival in Frankfurt with no arrival party or coordination.

On arrival in Frankfurt, both Leary and Harcourt were half awake and did not really fathom our predicament. For the past 18 months I had exchanged extensive information with German Customs. Most of that was regarding hashish shipments from Kabul to Germany. In doing so, I had learned the names of several German Customs officers. It was late at night in Frankfurt. I ran the names of the Customs officers I knew by the first officer we encountered. To my relief, I learned that Customs Agent Zimmerman was on duty on the midnight shift. I had met him personally on a previous stop in Frankfurt.

The first agent summoned Agent Zimmerman to us in the international lounge. I took Zimmerman aside, explained our dilemma, and requested medical assistance for Harcourt. Agent Zimmerman took us to an airport clinic where a doctor examined Harcourt. This was actually outside the official international area. Zimmerman took us there via a back route and we did not advise Leary of the detour. The doctor pronounced that Harcourt's hepatitis was beyond the communicative stage. According to him, she could still travel. The doctor gave her some vitamin shots and said she mainly needed rest. Agent Zimmerman then took us to the Pan Am Clipper Club Lounge in the International area. The lounge was closed for the night, but it was important that the pair remain in the international area. Otherwise they would be on German territory, which would raise new legal issues. Coincidentally, I was a member of the Clipper Club, but had never had the club opened just for my personal or professional use. Leary and Harcourt "crashed" on sofas. Agent Zimmerman got us some tea and blankets and left. He promised to return early in the morning prior to our flight to London. I sat on the floor with my back against the only exit door and tried to get some sleep.

The next morning we waited for our Pan Am flight that was coming from Beirut. I was busy changing our bookings. Harcourt asked me if she could borrow money to call her parents in London. The smallest U.S. currency I had was a $50 note that I gave her . . . and never got back. Instead of calling her parents, she called various London newspapers. Harcourt said she told the papers that she and Leary were being kidnapped, and they would be arriving in London in a few hours.

We were the only passengers in the first class section of the PAA flight from Frankfurt to London that morning of January 18, 1973. After getting airborne, Leary asked me if he and Harcourt could go up to the upper deck. I checked with the stewardess. She checked with the pilot who said they could. The cockpit door was locked and it was okay. I slumped into my seat and was quickly asleep.

Not for long, however. I was suddenly shaken awake by the stewardess who was half laughing. She said the Captain instructed that I had to get upstairs and "make them stop." "Stop what?" I asked. "Go see for yourself," she replied with a big grin. I ascended the spiral staircase to the upper deck. When my head reached the upper floor level I saw the bottoms of two pairs of feet facing me. The larger pair was inverted over the first. "Timothy," I said without climbing any further, "the pilot states that he will not allow this conduct on his aircraft. You have to stop. You are going to jail tonight so I'll give you five minutes to do so." Leary grunted his ascent and I returned to my seat and slumber.

Our arrival in London was tumultuous. We were met by London-based BNDD Agent Bill Collins and Frankfurt Agent Helmut Witt. They bulled our way through hoards of press to a VIP lounge. Leary was really enjoying the hoopla. He was not really complaining about his return to the U.S. That is, until a very officious British Foreign Office representative approached us. To my great dismay, the official asked Leary if he wished to request asylum in Great Britain. Leary immediately jumped on this and responded in the affirmative. He answered the questions regarding the basis for his request with great vigor. The official departed, promising an answer to the request prior to our scheduled departure. That was not to be for several hours.

During the wait, Leary and Harcourt hammed it up for the crowd and journalists. I just sat and stewed over British bureaucracy. The agony lasted until just moments before the plane was to depart. The self-important official finally arrived. He pompously announced that the request had been denied. As we walked to the departure gate, the official turned to me and whispered. "We had no intention of granting asylum, but we had to go through the motions." I told him could have saved me a lot of angst if he had told me that at the beginning.

The twelve hour Polar flight on Pan Am 121 was probably unlike any before or after in that first class section. Harcourt discovered that a fellow passenger was Opel automaker heir and playboy, Günter Sachs, who had attended boarding school with her in Switzerland. Sachs, his friends, and a couple of unrelated passengers, joined Leary and Harcourt on the upper deck. Harcourt produced a set of Tarot cards and soon the champagne was flowing. Even the stewardesses joined the fun. At one point Leary and Harcourt were sitting on the bulkhead couch. The others were playing with the cards on the floor in front of them. Harcourt stretched out on the couch with her head on Leary's lap. Leary reached down and unbuttoned the top button and pulled down the zipper of her jeans. Soon his hand was busy at play and Harcourt was verbalizing her enjoyment. A stewardess stood up. With great decorum, she covered Leary's hand and Harcourt's midsection with a blanket. The party went on.

I had been joined on the flight in London by another BNDD Agent, Vernon Stephens, who had come from our Paris office. He had been sent to London to give me a hand in case Leary, or anyone else, did something stupid on the flight. I welcomed his company as he was both smart and tough. I still had bad visions of some idiots on the plane attempting to rescue Leary. We spelled each other upstairs and down. Leary asked us if we would like to be police-men in his organization. We would police drug transac-tions so that no one would get "ripped off," he explained. We declined the offer.

Later in the flight I was in alone in the now almost empty lower section. Leary joined me there as we were passing over the ice cap. I pointed out to Leary that you could see the sun on the one side of the plane and the moon on the other. Leary agreed it was a great sight. It could be greatly improved though, he advised, if he had some acid to drop. Then, Leary did something he later regretted. It wasn't a violent move to escape. Leary asked me if I knew how he had escaped from the San Luis Obispo, Men's Correctional Prison. I told him that I did not, as I had actually never heard those details. Leary then related how he had made a hand-over-hand traverse of a tele-phone cable from a prison dormitory roof. Then he had climbed over the fence and crossed a perimeter road. Leary then described to me how he was picked up by Weather Underground terror organization members. They had taken Leary to a nearby gas station. There, according to Leary, Weatherman members had stashed civilian clothing in a trash can in the men's room. I allowed Leary to ramble on, providing more and more details of his escape. I had not placed him under arrest at any point in our journey; therefore, I had not warned him of his Miranda rights. Leary's bragging to me would later be challenged in court as to whether it had been a confession. Leary soon tired of his discourse and fell asleep. I had not taken any notes, not wanting to break the flow of his story or to have him see me doing so. I went into the toilet and wrote detailed notes about his confession.

When we arrived in Los Angeles the passengers were instructed to remain in their seats. Los Angeles BNDD Agent Don Strange and a Senior Supervisor, Howard Safir, came aboard with local officers. Leary was placed under arrest by California Bureau of Narcotics Agent Michael Barnes. Before he left the aircraft, I wished Leary well and then a weary Stephens and I stumbled off the aircraft. Only then did we see that the Los Angeles Police Department had gone all out to ensure that no person or group would affect a second escape of Leary. That would include the Weather Underground or anyone else. Heavily armed police lined the roof of the terminal. The terminal itself seemed to have more police present than passengers.

Two junior Los Angeles BNDD agents were nervously awaiting our arrival. Vern and I slumped into the back seat of their car for the ride to a downtown hotel. I felt no elation, only exhaustion. I knew I would just be given time to write my report before heading back to Kabul. One of the junior agents spoke up. "May I ask you a question? What is it like to be an international agent?" I laughed and told him that one simply needed to be able to go long stretches without sleep. That young agent, Craig Chretien, went on to have a very successful career that included international assignments in Peru and Brazil. Late in my career, when I was the Deputy Administrator of the DEA, Chretien became my Executive Assistant. He remains one of my closest friends.

While checking in at the hotel, I looked over at the newsstand. There, on the front page of the L.A. Times, was a large picture of my companions Leary and Harcourt and I arriving at Heathrow.

Chapter 25

I HAD ONLY BEEN BACK in Kabul for a few days when we developed information on a new drug laboratory. It was reported to be distilling opium to an oily state. The operators were also said to be extracting hashish oil from regular hashish. We conducted surveillance on the suspect location for several days. There were a number of male and female Westerners observed coming and going from the residence. On January 28, at my request, Afghan Police conducted a raid on the location. The suspect lab operation was there and was seized. In addition, there were suitcases in various stages of preparation for the concealment of opium oil. The operators had approximately $2,000 worth of electrical tools including sophisticated suture machines. There were supplies of epoxy resins and cloth for making polyethylene for false walls in the suitcases. A large supply of plywood for false walls in shipping crates was present. There were even diagrams showing false walled box construction. Several liters of opium oil and hashish were seized.

For me, the item of greatest interest was a document I discovered. It was a page from the January 4-5, 1972 meeting in San Francisco of the law enforcement BEL Task

Force. The page described my first investigation in Kabul, the Alexander Kulick case. A Jesse Arnold Katz and three colleagues at the lab site were arrested and charged. Katz would not speak to us.

There was someone waiting for me in Kabul who did want to talk. Dennis Martino had hooked back up with Leary and Harcourt in Beirut. There they had done various drugs for several days. It was Martino who suggested that they go to Afghanistan. There, he promised them, the main suppliers for BEL, The Tokhi brothers, would take care of them. Dennis Martino had evaded arrest when Timothy Leary and Joanna Harcourt had arrived in Kabul. Now Leary was back in prison and Harcourt somewhere in California. Martino was in Kabul, broke, hungry and strung out. He wanted to cooperate. A September 1975 Playboy article by Craig Vetter reported I had told Martino that he could only leave Afghanistan if he cooperated with the BNDD. Martino may have told Vetter or others that was true, but it was not. I spent three long days debriefing Martino. My report ran six, single spaced pages. I found that Martino was often fogged by drugs. When he wasn't; he was smart with an excellent memory.

I had learned a lot about the BEL over the last months. What Martino was telling me was ringing true. Martino had little tactical intelligence that I could use in Afghanistan. He did provide an historical perspective of BEL operations dating back to 1966. He first described the history of their LSD operations and then the development of the hashish operations beginning in 1968. He spoke of their relationship with the Tokhi brothers in Kandahar. He named names. Of interest to me was his detailed description of how hashish was distilled to hashish oil. He talked of the concealment methods they used in packages, vehicles, luggage, and shipping containers. He revealed methods used to counter "sniffer dogs" at airports and seaports. Martino described BEL's marijuana smuggling operations in Hawaii. They used a graceful 96' ocean going yacht. They packed and sealed cans labeled as health food with marijuana grown in Hawaii ("Maui Wowi"). These were then shipped on the yacht to the California. There, the marijuana was sold for $175 a pound. Martino said that in response to our January 1972 raid on the hashish factory run by Jacob Black and Saul Walters, BEL leader Bobby Andrist, sent an emissary to Afghanistan. The emissary met with Hayatullah Tokhi to teach him how to distill hashish. It was safer having the processing done in Kandahar than in Kabul.

Martino had knowledge of the whereabouts of a number of key BEL fugitives. That was of significance for BNDD in the United States. Some of them, according to Martino, were living on land in Chile, purchased by one of the BEL members. For others, he had exact addresses in places such as Michigan, Mexico, Newport Beach, Big Bear, California and Grants Pass, Oregon. My old fugitive, Rick Bevan, was living in Maui, Martino said. I immediately relayed this information to BNDD. A number of fugitive arrests occurred shortly thereafter.

I arranged for Martino's return to Los Angeles once I had wrung him dry of useful information. Martino provided some assistance to authorities there. At some point, his drug use and continuing antics with Harcourt rendered him virtually useless. Following Leary's escape trial, he provided a false statement to Leary's defense attorneys. He claimed that he had spied on the defense attorneys at Leary's trial on escape charges. He claimed that he had reported the defense's strategy to BNDD. That was totally false.

In March, 1975, Martino's body was discovered in a room in a cheap hotel in Marbella, Spain. A quarter empty bottle of Valium and a half bottle of wine were found in the room. That suggested to the Spanish authorities that Martino had died of an overdose. The coroner's report attributed his death to a ruptured appendix that caused gastritis and peritonitis. He was 29 years old. His twin brother, David, had followed a similar path of drug destruction and committed suicide in 1984.

Chapter 26

IN MARCH, AMBASSADOR NEUMANN REQUESTED that I travel to Bangkok to meet with U.N. officials and U.S. Embassy counter narcotics personnel. At issue was whether the Kabul Embassy should back the UN narcotics plan being proposed for Afghanistan. The plan copied that which the U.N. had implemented in Thailand. Ambassador Neumann wanted to know if the plan could really be applied to Afghanistan. Irene took a well deserved break from Kabul to accompany me.

The day before our return to Kabul I received a cable from BNDD Headquarters. I was to travel immediately to San Luis Obispo, California. I was to testify there at the escape trial of Timothy Leary. Irene and I split up at the Bangkok Airport. I headed east on TWA and she headed west on Pakistan International Airlines (PIA). Hers was a harrowing trip. After changes in Karachi and Islamabad, she had arrived late in Peshawar. She had just missed her flight from Peshawar to Kabul. She was told by the airlines that there would be no flight for days. At her hotel there was a Kabul businessman in the same dilemma. He had rented a taxi to drive him to Kabul the next day and had found two other Afghans to share the cost. He invited Irene to do the same. Irene endured a long trip through the Khyber Pass jammed in between her fellow passengers. They stopped several times at roadside shacks to purchase tea. As a woman, Irene could not join them. It was a heck of a trip.

I, meanwhile, had gotten lucky. Before lifting off from Bangkok, one of the TWA stewards and I recognized each other; we had crossed paths on an earlier U.S. domestic flight. I had been armed on that trip. Per protocol, I had identified myself to the crew. He asked where I was headed for and I told him I was going all the way to Los Angeles. He excused himself and went forward. He came back and told me to grab my gear; the captain had kindly invited me to take a seat in the first class cabin. When we landed in Hong Kong the steward advised there was a crew change there. For security reasons, the old crew had no contact with the oncoming crew and he could not advise the new crew of my status. He had no idea how many first class passengers were boarding. "Good luck", he said in parting. The aircraft was a Boeing 707 with only ten seats in first class. I was in the back aisle window seat. I pulled a blanket around me and feigned sleep. The new crew and then the new passengers came aboard. There were nine passengers, several were couples traveling together. Under slit eyes I watched as they re-arranged the cabin seating around me.

The cabin crew explained to the new folks that there must have been a mistake in the seating arrangements. I enjoyed the rest of the trip.

On arrival in Los Angeles, I rented a car and drove up the coast to San Luis Obispo. I checked in at the Sheriff's office. Sheriff Larry Mansfield was very welcoming and assigned two deputies to look after me. Learning that I was traveling without a weapon, he immediately loaned me one. Mansfield was concerned about what some of Leary's colleagues might try. My stay was on the Sheriff's Department. The two deputies and I enjoyed a great dinner overlooking the ocean. The next morning was the opening of the trial. Joana Harcourt was present in the hall outside the courtroom. She looked so down that I passed on reminding her that she owed me $50 from her Frankfurt phone calls. There was a motley crew of Leary devotees in the hallways and courtroom. Their enthusiasm waned as the trial ran into a long second week.

I testified as to the return of Leary from Kabul. Out of jury testimony was necessary at several points. This bench-only testimony was in response to Leary's counsel's claim. Lawyer Bruce Margolis charged that I had kidnapped Leary and Leary should not even be before the court. Judge Richard F. Harris was a quiet, but very strong presence in the courtroom. He ruled that on a certain date Leary was in the legal custody of the state. Leary had then removed himself from that custody without authority. Leary was now back in legal custody. It really didn't matter to Judge Harris how Leary had gotten to his courtroom. There were factors that seemed to sway the judge to that decision. If I had kidnapped Leary, then why spend $1,000 of U.S. Government funds to bring Harcourt back as well? How many kidnappees were treated to first class air travel? How many companions of kidnappees received medical attention during their travel? It took time, but the right decision came down.

Another very large issue was that of whether I had placed Leary under arrest when we left Kabul. Had I coerced the confession that he had made to me regarding how he had escaped? And, were his statements regarding the assistance of his family and the Weather Underground coerced? Leary was now allowed to join his flamboyant Attorney, Bruce Margolin, in cross examining me. My testimony had been that Leary gave me the details of his escape voluntarily. This Leary challenged. I was asked how I could remember such details. "Had I taken notes"? "Yes" I replied. "Where are those notes?" "I attached them to the case file folder in the Los Angeles BNDD office after writing my official report". Margolin demanded that I produce those notes. Judge Harris instructed me to have them brought to the court. We recessed.

That evening, a BNDD agent drove the notes from Los Angeles. Meanwhile, Prosecutor Robert Lilley and his two

Paso Robles detectives and I relaxed with a drink and dinner. Having always viewed the courtroom as a drama stage, I enjoyed Lilley's stories. His regular courtroom beat was Paso Robles. That was a several hour drive over a major ridge to the north. That was cattle country before it became wine country. There, many of his prosecutions were for cattle theft. In the Paso Robles court he always wore the ill fitting suit he had graduated from high school in. It was an oft-pressed suit with short cuffs. He would always wear cowboy boots. Lilley talked in a homey language to the Paso Robles juries. That went over well in the north side of "The Ridge". In this San Luis Obispo courtroom, he was a polished, articulate, and immaculately dressed prosecutor. He could challenge the best Los Angeles attorney money could buy.

The next morning, defense attorney Margolis exploded from his seat towards the witness stand. "Agent Burke", he demanded, "Can you present your notes to this court?" "Yes sir", I responded, but without moving. "Would the Court please instruct Agent Burke to produce his notes?" requested Margolis. Judge Harris prompted, "Agent Burke?" "Your honor", said I, while reaching to my inside suit coat pocket. The previously very carefully accordion folded toilet paper length emerged from my pocket. I held it in the air in front of me, raising it until the last fold emerged. It took Judge Harris several poundings of his gavel to reduce the laughter in the court to a reasonable level. Even the staid judge cracked a smile. I did not. "Would Agent Burke please explain the nature of his notes?" the judge intoned. I explained that I had not sought Leary's description of his escape. Nor had I questioned him regarding the details he had provided. Because I had recognized the significance of his dialogue, I had not wanted to interrupt its flow by taking notes. I had waited therefore, until he had run out of information and had fallen asleep. I had a pen, but no paper of the necessary quantity to write on. I had, therefore, retired to the toilet and inscribed my notes on the presented length of toilet paper. "No further questions", a now very quiet Margolin advised.

After about ten days I was finally free to go. The California Attorney General's office wanted me to fly to Zurich and interview Leary's former wife, Rosemary. There was considerable legal controversy over that idea. BNDD Headquarters said they would seek a final decision. I should proceed in that direction and they would contact me at JFK Airport prior to my boarding the flight to Zurich. I missed their page there (it was very noisy in the bar). On arrival in Zurich, I checked in with the Embassy in Bern. An anxious official informed me that they had tried to reach me in New York to tell me that I should not contact Rosemary under any circumstances. Pity, here I was in Zurich with no onward flight to Tehran, the next stop, for a couple of days. Sheriff Mansfield had told me not to worry about the cost of the trip. They were happy to get Leary back and they credited me for that. I really enjoyed the five stars Dolder Grand Hotel overlooking Zurich.

Arriving in Tehran, I found I had a three day wait until the next flight to Kabul. I rented a taxi, and drove 45 miles north into the Alborz Mountain Range. There, I enjoyed great spring skiing at Dizin, the Shah's ski resort. My last night in Tehran I enjoyed Beluga caviar and fine champagne. I toasted Leary for his choice to go to Kabul. At almost that same time, the jury in San Luis Obispo was finding Leary guilty of escape. They had taken less than two hours to deliberate. Judge Harris gave him six months to five years for the escape. Leary was also facing serious time for other charges.

Chapter 27

BACK IN KABUL, THE BUREAUCRATIC side of BNDD's
responsibilities rose to the fore. It was time to prepare "The
Outlook for Implementation of the Narcotics Program for
Afghanistan". I had contributed significantly to the plan.
That didn't mean I really believed in a successful outcome
for the plan, however. I had attempted to hedge all bets in
my contribution. My report reflected that. It was not that
the Embassy held out a cheery picture either. There was not
a more practical diplomat than U.S. Ambassador Neumann,
nor one who worked harder to get a host government moving in the right direction. The rest of his "Country Team" followed suit. As I wrote my report, news from the Palace was
received. King Zahir had just enacted the "Afghan Police
Law" by royal decree. Twelve years in the drafting, the law
finally gave legitimate status to the Afghan Police. It was a
glimmer of progress.

That progress was immediately offset by the Ministry of
the Interior's news. As threatened by Hakkim, they removed
narcotics investigation responsibility from the Criminal
Investigation Division of the Police. The order fragmented
the responsibility within three uncoordinated elements in

the Ministry. Adding to the dilemma was Prime Minister Shafiq's appointment of a new narcotics coordinator. Dr. Sayed Abdul Quader Baha was the former Director of Kabul University. While he was an able school administrator, he admittedly knew nothing of narcotics.

Even the United Nations got into the act. Their very able Enforcement Advisor, Mervin Mandy, informed the Afghan Government that their draft narcotics law was totally unacceptable. In addition, it was completely contrary to all advice provided by the UN. In April, 1973, I suggested in my report to BNDD the possibility that the Shafiq government could fall. I had no idea of how far Shafiq's fall would be later that summer.

In late April 1973, Agent Mike Holm and I developed an investigation that had serious political implications. One of our long standing and trusted sources of information had been approached by an Afghan, Rajib Ali. Ali wanted our source to locate a buyer in California for 88 pounds of hashish oil. Ali informed our man that he was distilling the hashish for Mohammed Rahim Panshiri. The political problem was that Panshiri was one of the most powerful men in Afghanistan and in the royal palace. Panshiri was also known as "Bacha Rahim". He was said to be the bastard son of King Nadir Shah, the father of the present King Zahir. That would make him a stepbrother to King Zahir. He was referred to as the valet to the King, but his position was of much greater power. Also of political significance to the case was that Panshiri planned to ship the liquid hashish as part of a diplomatic shipment of unidentified goods. The shipment was destined for the Royal Afghan Embassy in Washington, D.C..

Ali told the source that Panshiri wanted the sale to take place in California. That would be as far away from the Embassy in Washington as possible. Panshiri, according to Ali, expected to make $500,000 from the shipment. A third of that allegedly would go to Ali and our source. Over the next weeks, the plans for the shipment continued to evolve. Details regarding the amount to be shipped and the types of containers to be used changed often. The routing for the shipment remained to be through the Afghan Embassy in Washington. Suddenly, however, everything went quiet regarding Panshiri's plans.

The interruption was probably due to a seizure based on information from Germany that I passed to Samad Azhar in Kabul. This time it was not a shipment of drugs, however. It was, of all things, 4,400 pounds of hard core pornographic playing cards. The BNDD office in Frankfurt, Germany had been coordinating with us regarding shipments of hashish into Germany from Afghanistan. In late May, the Frankfurt agents notified me that four crates of the playing cards were en route to Kabul. German authorities suspected the cards were payment for hashish that had been shipped from Afghanistan. The crates were addressed to, "Private Secretary, Arig-I-Shahi"; the Royal Palace. All pornography was against Shari Law and banned in Afghanistan.

The shipment was due on an incoming Ariana Airlines flight. I immediately advised Samad Azhar of the information. He located and seized the shipment. Azhar asked me to put the information in writing. This I did on plain bond paper with no attribution. A few days later, I held a clandestine meeting with Azhar. As strong a man as he was, he was shaken by the situation. He genuinely feared for his life because he had stopped the shipment. He had determined that the cards were intended for members of HRM King Zahir's personal security force. He confirmed the German's suspicion that the shipment was payment for shipments of drugs to Germany. The shipment remained under Azhar's control at the airport. But, he could not take normal contraband seizure action because of who was involved.

Azhar said he had turned my sterile memo over to His Royal Highness, Prince Sardar Sultan Mahmud Ghazi. Sultan Ghazi was President of the Afghan Air Authority and first cousin to the King. Sultan Ghazi told Azhar he had turned my memo over to King Zahir, who would "look into it". Both Ghazi and the King had been advised that I had authored the memorandum. Because I was identified as the source of the information that led to the seizure,

Azhar warned that I should expect retaliation because my role was now known.

Two days later, Azhar requested that I meet with him and Prince Sultan Ghazi. This we did in a private location. Ghazi was a handsome, well educated man. He informed me that he was meeting with me at the direction of King Zahir. Ghazi said that it had been determined that the shipment had been intended for Panshiri. The King had been upset over a New York Times article on May 24, 1973. The Times reported that the Royal household was involved in smuggling activities. Ghazi stated that my information a few days later about the cards proved the story true. He said "they" need my help in firming the case against Panshiri. This would not be a situation that would be handled in the courts, however. King Zahir, according to Ghazi, knew he had to take action to stop Panshiri's activity. He reminded me that Panshiri was very powerful, "He selects the ministers," Ghazi said.

I briefed Ghazi on the details of the shipment as we knew them. I identified the two names given to the airlines as the shippers. One of them, Ali Rahimi Ghazi, was identified as Panshiri's son. I suggested that Ghazi request the German Government to interrogate the shippers. They should obtain statements from them as to the sponsor of the project. I offered to alert the German Government to his request. Ghazi said he would follow that course. He asked that I provide him with an official report on the smuggling operation. I agreed to do so and then I told Ghazi of other smuggling acts by Palace staff. I explained how staff used official trips and the King's aircraft to smuggle drugs abroad. The information was sobering, but not a surprise to Ghazi. He and I discussed further the drug situation in Afghanistan. I expressed my frustration that Azhar was the only Afghan police officer I could trust. He was the only one to take positive action on information I supplied. Ghazi asked for details of the recent seizure in Iran of 12.6 tons of Afghan opium. I had the names of the sources of the opium and agreed to provide them to him.

Ghazi closed the meeting stating he would inform King Zahir of the details. He reiterated that those involved were very powerful and that they would learn of my involvement. He cautioned me to be very careful. I gave Azhar a ride back to the airport. I learned that he had told Ghazi of the shipment as soon as he had located it. Ghazi had instructed him to keep the seizure a secret until he informed the King. The next day, two Palace officials came to the airport. They inspected and sealed the entire shipment with the Palace seal.

I later learned that the entire playing card shipment had been "destroyed". Rajib Ali broke contact with our informant in the proposed hash oil operation. Panshiri went to ground. A few months later he traveled with the

King to Rome. This was just prior to the coup d'état by Daoud Khan on July 17, 1972. Subsequent to the coup d'état, Panshiri's house was searched and liquid hashish and other drugs were found. Panshiri eventually returned to Afghanistan. He was arrested there following the 1978 Peoples Democratic Party of Afghanistan (PDPA....Afghan Communist Party) coup d'état that ousted Daoud. There was irony in his arrest; Samad Azhar was one of the leaders of the PDPA coup and, by then, the Police Deputy Inspector General.

Chapter 28

MY MEETINGS WITH EUGENE CHAPLIGIN of the Soviet Embassy had continued throughout the spring of 1973. I had developed additional information on various smuggling routes through the Soviet Union that I shared with him. I was quite surprised at the news he brought to a meeting in early May. He told me that his government was extending an invitation for me to make an official visit to Moscow. The Soviet Main Customs Administration was very concerned about my reports of smuggling through the USSR. They wished to hear the facts directly from me. Chapligin thought that they were also ready to establish the enhanced liaison relationship I had requested. I had found that Chapligin was not always available when I had perishable information to pass which was often time sensitive. It could be regarding an imminent shipment, or persons leaving for Moscow with drugs. I needed to be able to talk to someone who could act on the information immediately. Chapligin said that USSR Customs was ready to discuss this with me.

I cleared the trip through BNDD Headquarters, the State Department, and the U.S. Embassy in Moscow. The

Embassy there was recovering from President Nixon's just completed trip to Moscow. Now they were very busy preparing for Soviet President Leonid Brezhnev's scheduled June 18 state visit to Washington. Despite that conflict, they were more than willing to approve my visit. Apparently, they welcomed any opportunity for cooperation with the Soviets. During President Nixon's visit, there had of course been Secret Service Agents accompanying him. However, as far as the Embassy knew, mine would be the first visit of a U.S. Federal Agent in an official liaison capacity.

I flew out of Kabul on an Aeroflot flight to Moscow that changed aircraft in Tashkent. In the Kabul departure area I had noticed two Western men and one woman. All three appeared to be in their twenties. They wore semi hippie garb, but were neat and clean. I saw that the luggage they checked seemed to be of good quality. We had a couple of hour layover in Tashkent. This was the first entry point in the USSR, so you showed your passport there. I maneuvered to get behind one of the Western men in the passport line. I had noted in the Kabul Airport that the other two seemed to defer to him. He placed his open passport on the counter and I was able to see that it was an American passport and I could read his name. I heard him explain to the Soviet Immigration official that he was only transiting the USSR and did not require a visa.

There was no food served on the Kabul to Tashkent leg and no meals on the very long, 1,750 mile Tashkent to Moscow leg. The aircraft to Moscow was a four engine propeller model that was no speeding rocket. To make up for the lack of airborne food service, they fed you in Tashkent. I was fortunate to grab a chair at the table next to the three Americans. When I heard them conversing in English, I joined in. They asked me where I was headed and I said to Moscow and then connecting to London and New York. I was cagey and acted as though I was avoiding talking about the purpose of my travel. I asked if they had made the trip before. They assured me they had, many times. I started inquiring whether anyone was searched in Moscow or in London. They picked up on this and the fact that I was appearing a bit nervous. We shared a couple of beers. I allowed that I was carrying some "gifts" for friends. The route had been recommended to me as one where I wouldn't have "problems". I was concerned however, as it was my first time using the route. I was unsure of what to expect and noted that I didn't want to become a "guest" of the Soviets.

By that time they were smiling to each other about this dolt who probably would get caught. Then they became my "counselors". I was told to stay in the international lounge in Moscow. I was taking a big chance in London and New York. Customs in both places would see from my passport that I had come from Kabul. I needed to do what they always did. Shortly after our arrival in Moscow, there was a connecting flight to East Berlin. They even gave me the flight number. According to them, East Berlin authorities never checked anyone coming from Moscow. They then gave me details of how to leave the East Berlin Airport and catch a taxi to the subway station near the Brandenburg Gate. There was a West Berlin subway that operated in the Western Sector, but transited a small section of the Soviet Sector near the Gate. The subway stopped there and non-Germans could get on and off the trains. The subway then re-entered West Berlin where there were no checks of the passengers. There were no checks because the U.S. and the Allies refused to recognize sector lines as borders. My "counselors" then mailed their "Afghan gifts" from West Berlin to the U.S. On previous trips, their packages had not been checked in the U.S. post offices due their West German origin. I was so grateful for their guidance that I paid the tab for all of the beers.

After a long night's flight, we arrived at Sheremetyvo Airport in Moscow. During the night, I had told my new friends that I didn't have enough money to change my itinerary. Because they had made me aware of the risk I was taking, I had dumped my "gifts" into the toilet on the plane. They were small gifts this time and there was no great loss. The next time I would follow their route. In Moscow, I made sure they did not see me exiting the airport.

I caught a taxi to the huge Hotel Rossiya on Red Square across from the Kremlin. This was an ugly cement 21 storey monster with 3,200 rooms. There were four wings on each floor. In the center of each wing was a large desk. The desk on my floor and wing was manned at all times. The clerks must have been selected from the nastiest women in the USSR. The room keys hung on large board behind them. Each key was connected to a wooden ball that was large enough to ensure you would not walk out of the hotel with it. They did not speak English or me, Russian. On reaching the desk, I would write my room number down. They would reach behind them, search the board and then thump a key on the desk in front of me. They would give me a nasty glare and turn their backs. The room was narrow with one single bed, but it had a fairly large window that opened and provided a pleasant view of the Moscow River. This would be my home for eight days. My meeting with the Soviets was on Tuesday, but the next flight back to Kabul was not until the following Tuesday.

It was Sunday, so I called my Embassy contact, Jack Tech, at home. I told him I had to send an urgent cable to our BNDD Agent in Bonn. Jack picked me up a short time later and took me to the Embassy. I sent an "immediate" cable off to Bonn, asking that they notify the West German Police of the expected arrival in Berlin of the party of three. They would be on the subway from East

Berlin that evening. I provided names and detailed physical and clothing descriptions. Tech then drove me back to the hotel. He and his wife picked me up that evening and hosted me to an excellent dinner in a Georgian restaurant. Late on Monday, we were advised that the three Americans had been arrested by the West German Police at the West German subway station. They had a good number of pounds of Afghan hashish concealed in the sides of their suitcases. I was pleased to have identified another smuggling route. I also planned to use the incident as a talking point with the Soviets.

On Tuesday morning, Jack Tech picked me up and we drove to the Main Soviet Customs building. There we met with Main Customs Deputy Chiefs, Edward G. Ivanov and Viktor G. Kalantarov. Both were in brown uniforms with epaulets on their broad shoulders and medals on their expansive chests. There was a third man present in a dark civilian suit. He was not identified nor did he ever leave his seat. He did not acknowledge my attempt at a handshake, nor did he ever speak throughout the meeting. A lady who spoke excellent English served as interpreter. Ivanov's office was large and high ceilinged, but heavily curtained and dark. He sat behind a massive desk, behind which hung a large red Soviet flag. It was a relatively bare room, but still imposing. We started off with my providing them with a number of briefing documents. First, was a report I had prepared titled, "Potential Smuggling Routes from Afghanistan and Pakistan through the USSR to Europe and The United States." In two other reports I provided the identities and details of Afghans believed to be using the routes. It also gave facts of their concealment methods. A BNDD organizational chart and the BNDD 1972 annual report were given to them. The last item was an illustrated guide to concealment locations for contraband in Mercedes-Benz sedans.

I then told them of my contact with the three Americans on my flight. I described what had drawn my attention to them and the subterfuge I had employed to gain their confidence. I laid out in detail the smuggling route the trio had described to me. I concluded by telling Ivanov and Kalantarov that I would have liked to have provided them with the information. Because we had not yet had this meeting however, I had not been able to do so. Instead, the West German Police had made the arrests and drug seizure. Ivanov and Kalantarov expressed disappointment that they had not been able to get the information. Jack Tech looked like he was relieved that the Embassy had not had to deal with three American citizens being arrested in Moscow.

Ivanov and Kalantarov received the briefing and the documents with obvious interest and enthusiasm. Tech noted later that there had been none of the stiffness and reserve in the meeting that was the norm for U.S. Embassy-Soviet exchanges. Ivanov advised that they had not been previously aware of the transit trafficking problem. They would now explore it fully. He promised to honor my request that a Soviet representative in Kabul be identified. This would be someone to whom I could pass "tactical" intelligence. In the meantime, he asked that I pass information to him through Tech. This was to avoid the information getting lost in the Ministry of Foreign Affairs, he said. Ivanov said that any information available from BNDD would be welcomed by his government. He acknowledged what he called the USSR's developing problem with drugs. I described the BNDD international training program to him and suggested that both governments give consideration to having BNDD provide introductory narcotics training to the Soviet Police and Customs. Both Ivanov and Kalantarov appeared to welcome the suggestion.

I told them that some of the Afghans identified in the briefing material regularly transited the USSR en route to Europe. In Europe they would collect payment for their drugs and arrange for future shipments. For the Afghans, flying the USSR route was much cheaper than the southern route. I suggested that Ivanov's people might want to keep an eye on them when they stopped over in Moscow as they might be looking for a market in the USSR. Ivanov leaned his very stout body over the desk. He declared, "When they come here we will know how many strokes they take when they brush their teeth". I stifled the thought of asking him how many strokes I used.

I also suggested that they begin to develop sources at the Afghan/Soviet border crossings where the containers transferred to Soviet control. There was a good chance that Afghan truck drivers would have an idea of which of the containers they had carried had been handled in Kabul in a suspicious manner. For a reasonable stipend they might be willing to anonymously share that information.

I advised that it would be helpful if I could see suspect Aeroflot freight waybills in Kabul. I could then provide them with information on the shippers and European recipients. I would expect that our liaison would include the Soviets providing me feedback on the results of their searches and inquiries. Ivanov assured me that would take place. They would absorb my information and respond to my request for a counterpart in Kabul. The meeting ended on a most cordial note. I mentioned to them that I hoped to see the Bolshoi Ballet if it was in season and the Moscow Circus during the week ahead. I was disappointed to learn that I would not be able to do so. I was in Moscow as an official visitor they informed me. I was not a tourist and I had not gone to the USSR through Intourist, the official Soviet travel agency. Without the required Intourist card, I could not get tickets for any of the main Moscow attractions. Ah, we aren't the only bureaucratic country, I thought.

Jack Tech had to get back to his real job so he dropped me at the Rossiya. I wanted to celebrate what I considered a personal breakthrough in US/Soviet relations. I just didn't know where to go to celebrate. Wandering into the massive lobby I discovered a gift shop. I bought the two items I needed. A jar of caviar and a six pack of Carlsberg Beer. I sat in the open window of my room that evening and enjoyed both. The only problem I had was that I could not buy or borrow a spoon in the hotel to eat the caviar with. It turned out the metal pull tab on the beer can served that purpose. I even managed not to cut my tongue.

The rest of the week was mild. I rose early each morning and mapped out my walk for the day. I'd try to pick out a place I wanted to visit that was about a two hour walk from the hotel, just to kill time. I wandered through department stores, and spent a lot of time in war museums. In one department store I was treated to a most unusual display. There was a table about 30 feet long just in front of the entrance. On the table was row after row of brassieres. They were in an ascending order in size from left to right; each size stacked about a dozen high. By the time I reached the far end of the table, the bras were so large they stretched credibility. On Thursday afternoon the sun was warm. I was walking through a park along the Moscow River; I stopped, stretched out on the grass, and dozed off. The next thing I knew, someone had delivered a hard blow to the sole of my shoe. I looked up to see two stout Moscow matrons standing over me, scowling. I didn't need to speak Russian to understand they were not pleased with my napping in the park. When I later described the incident to Jack Tech, he howled. The Moscow Mayor had just initiated a drive against public intoxication. The two ladies had obviously interpreted my sleeping and prone position in the grass as representative of that prohibited behavior.

I jogged around the Revolution Square and down into its famous metro station. I bought post cards of Red Square and the Kremlin. In my room I addressed them to various old colleagues in the States, but did not sign them or provide a return address. I wrote the same message on each of them; "From Russia with Love". I'm sure some of the recipients spent time checking them for micro dots or turned them over to their security office at work. On Thursday evening I discovered the Embassy's in-house bar managed by the U.S. Marine Security Detachment. When I told the Marine bartender that I had served as a Marine Guard in the Rome Embassy early in my career, I was immediately afforded carte blanche to the place. This must have been one of the world's super watering holes. Western journalists, friendly foreign embassy personnel, lonely Embassy single male and female staff, and married Embassy staff crowded the long bar. It must have been a KGB penetration target of the highest order. After a few evenings there I think

I heard about everything going on in the Embassy. Not to mention, who was sleeping with whom. The Marines were the bartenders and the drinks were cheap.

By Saturday, I was going stir crazy. In going to Moscow I had a concern. From their infamous modus operandi I knew there was the chance that the Soviets might attempt to compromise me for black mail purposes. With that in mind, I had been very careful in entering my room each night. I'd open the door, reach in and turn on the ceiling light. I'd then say something like, "I know you are in there, it won't work!" By Saturday night I was so bored I opened the door a crack and slid into the room without touching the light. I threw myself on the bed saying, "Take me!" That didn't work either.

On Sunday, winter returned to Moscow, at least judging by the temperature. On Sundays, The Kremlin Museums were open to the public. I crossed Red Square towards Lenin's Tomb where the nattily uniformed Guards goosed-stepped with great precision. The entrance to the Kremlin for the tours was a small wooden door in the huge stone wall just to the right of the Tomb. When I got there the line was about ten persons wide. It stretched halfway across Red Square. I joined the queue on the rear and far left of the line. This way I was able to kill time by watching the Tomb Guards. Soon, many others joined the line behind me. It was getting colder and colder. All week I had wondered if

I had been under surveillance, but I had not seen any sign, although I had made no attempt to check for it. After about two hours in the line, I got my confirmation. I was tapped on the shoulder from behind. A very large man in a civilian coat and hat was standing there; he looked as cold as I felt. He motioned me to follow him. I did and we walked the still significant distance to the door in the wall. There, two uniformed guards checked everyone's identification. My new friend flashed credentials to the guards, he was saluted in return and the door was opened for us. Inside, he turned and gave me a small wave while he headed for the coffee shop and I for the exhibits.

I returned to the Rossiya for lunch. The restaurant was cavernous. The tables were empty except for the one I was led to. There sat a thin, very elderly, white haired gentleman. He had a sash across the front of the suit, denoting some honor and a few ribboned medals pinned to his jacket. I sat down and we exchanged nods. The waitress who had seated me retreated to side wall and resumed her conversation with several other servers. She had not provided me with a menu, so I attempted to signal my request for one from across the room. No response. The gentleman shook his head like, "Don't expect anything". He lifted the vodka bottle in front of him, reached across the table with a shaky hand, and filled my glass. "Vashe zdorovie", said he. It took a very long time to get served by the waitress, but not by the gentleman. We had no conversation; he just kept pouring the vodka. I finally ate "something", went to my room and took a long nap.

Two more evening stops at the Marine Bar and I was out of Moscow. The flight back was through the night. At one point I awoke and headed for the toilet. I walked right by it in the dim light. Ahead of me was a bulkhead across what must have been the rear quarter of the plane.

There was a door in the center that I opened; inside was quite a scene. There were living room style chairs and a couch across the back bulkhead, not the butt breaking seats as in the rest of the aircraft. Empty vodka bottles were strewn about the carpeted floor. About six Russian male passengers and three of the stewardesses were in various stages of undress and activity on the furniture and the floor. "I guess there is a first class section on this flight after all", I thought to myself as I closed the door. A laughing stewardess emerged from the rear section. As she buttoned her blouse she smiled and pointed out the toilet.

Not long after my return to Kabul, Chapligin told me that he was leaving Kabul for a new assignment. At the direction of Moscow, my new liaison was to be the Kabul Aeroflot Manager. The manager was a very tall, beautiful, raven haired lady. She always caused a stir among the men every time she walked through the airport. I had Tasha checked out by our Embassy and learned that she was the wife of the Soviet Embassy KGB Rezidentura, the chief of the local KGB. Tasha was also considered to be a KGB agent. True to their word, the Customs officials in Moscow had arranged that Tasha was authorized to accept and exchange information with me. We met at the airport over the next weeks on a number of occasions. This was usually the day before the weekly Aeroflot flight to Moscow. Tasha would show me the manifest and passport information for the non-Russian passengers. I would check for any potential suspects and advise her of any who appeared to warrant a check in Tashkent or Moscow. Tasha was always very professional, but she had a great sense of humor and I enjoyed working with her. The Embassy political officers could not resist tossing jealousy-driven jokes my way over the liaison.

Tasha and I had several successful seizures for our efforts. The Soviet officials generally just confiscated the drugs when there were relatively small amounts. They fined the culprit on the spot, and let them leave Moscow on their connecting flight. This was okay with the U.S. Embassy in Moscow. Dealing with arrested Americans there was a nightmare for them.

Containers were a different problem. It was difficult for me to identify specific containers that were being used to transit the USSR with drugs. I had to rely on providing Tasha with names of suspect Afghan shippers and suspect recipients in Europe. My description of the routes and players did allow European authorities to make several seizures. It certainly alerted the Soviet officials to the problem. That was later evidenced by the arrest of three Americans at Moscow's Sheremetyvo Airport in 1976. The three Americans were caught transiting from Kuala Lumpur to Amsterdam with 62 pounds of heroin hidden in their suitcases. They did not get a slap on the wrist, they received long prison sentences.

It turned out that my attempt to initiate a training program by BNDD for the Soviets went for naught. On July 1, 1973, BNDD became the Drug Enforcement Administration (DEA). The Administration had created the new agency by merging the narcotics investigators of the U.S. Customs Service with the BNDD Agents. Thus, they created the new agency. The Headquarters elements were all merged in the BNDD Headquarters at 14th and Eye Streets N.W. in Washington, D.C. Most folks there were too busy wrestling over titled positions and corner offices to pay attention to what some guy in Kabul was trying to do. The liaison effort with Tasha continued up to my departure. My replacement did not arrive for several months later. He declared that he was not going to work with, "A bunch of Commies" and the liaison operation died on the vine. The Soviets solved the entire Afghan-USSR drug transit problem by invading Afghanistan in 1979.

Chapter 29

MY CONTACT WITH SENIOR AFGHAN officials continued to escalate during the summer of 1973. My meetings with senior Afghan officials did not bother Ambassador Neumann nor his Deputy, Sam Lewis. There was one or two in the Embassy's Political Section who appeared to think I was treading on their turf. Ambassador Neumann always turned the argument around on the players. If they were not successful in developing these confidences, was it not to the benefit of the Embassy that someone else was able to do so?

A year before, I had been able to indirectly assist one very senior Afghan official. He had a problem involving his son in India. My contact with the CBI resolved the problem. A mutual trust with the official had developed as the result. The man was one of Afghanistan's only qualified jurists. He had served in numerous international positions. He held an M.A. and PhD from a prestigious Western University. The official told me that he felt the U.S. had made a fatal mistake in basing its narcotics programs on assurances of Prime Minister Shafiq. He said that, prior to being named as Prime Minister, Shafiq made statements based on what he thought the U.S. wanted to hear. In turn, the U.S. backed Shafiq with the King. That caused the King to name Shafiq as Prime Minister. The official cited examples from Shafiq's history as a corrupt and venal individual. He cited examples of his corruption. He said the second factor against Shafiq was his family, principally his father. That man owned some of the largest opium producing land in Afghanistan. The official went on to cite other powerful individuals who were involved in narcotics trafficking. Not surprising, they included Palace power, Rahim Panshiri and Parliamentarian Qadus Mahmood.

A not so cordial meeting took place a few days later with Samiuddin Zhouand, Deputy Minister of Justice. Zhouand said he was meeting me at the request of Prime Minister Shafiq. Zhouand made all sorts of positive pronouncements regarding cooperation in drug cases. What he was really after, though, was something else. He wanted everything we had on Afghan Parliamentarians and other officials. In diplomatic terms, I told him no. Instead, I suggested, we should concentrate on the cases I had already identified to the Afghans and, for which there had been no action to date. It became obvious that Zhouand was strictly fishing for information. He could use the information as leverage against the people he wanted me to identify. His tactic didn't work. It was clear when we concluded the meeting that he was not happy with the results.

In late June, I wrote a strong memo to BNDD Headquarters. The memo reported the difficulties they could expect in seeing the Afghan Narcotics Program carried out. I urged that an agreement be forged between my office, our Ankara Regional Office and Headquarters. The objective was to have a common policy to be pursued by all of those elements. I urged speedy action as I would be departing Kabul in late July and there would soon be a new Agent in Charge in Kabul. Apparently they were busy playing reorganizational musical chairs in Washington, D.C., as I never received a response.

I had one of my last forays undercover in Kabul in July. What occurred caused me to conclude that my luck there was running out. I had gone with a German informant into a large walled compound just outside of Kabul. The German Police Advisor had just turned the informant over to me. The Germans wanted our new target, Haji Firuz Khan, taken down as he was moving large amounts of hashish and morphine tablets to Germany. The informant said that Khan would expect me to smoke a sample of the hashish and opium he was offering for sale. To avoid this, I feigned a sore throat and started coughing from the time I passed the armed guards at the compound entrance. The ruse worked, but Khan insisted that the informant try the drugs. Negotiating with Khan was very awkward as he had only one eye. His blind, left eye was lodged permanently to the side of the socket with the pupil appearing to be constantly peering over his left shoulder. His right eye stared straight ahead. When speaking to him, you tended to want to follow the blind gaze of the left eye to see what it was that he was "staring at" over his shoulder. It was very disconcerting.

After puffing on a hashish joint, the informant really screwed up the situation. He started asking Khan why he seemed so paranoid. Khan replied that the American Interpol Agent at the U.S. Embassy had been causing the traffickers a lot of problems. In the past, there was little chance of arrest because you just paid off the police. Now the American was forcing the authorities to take action. The informant and I were sitting on an old ragged carpet over the dirt floor of the room. Khan was standing, pacing back and forth. Three guards with rifles stood at the edge of the room. Now the German made a bad situation even worse. He asked what Khan knew of the American "Interpol" Agent. Khan claimed that they watched him all the time. They even had a photo of him from the American magazine *Newsweek*. The agent had captured someone and taken him to prison in the U.S. "What does he look like?" asked the German. "Well", said Khan, "he is tall, like your friend there. He has dark hair and a beard like him, pretty much the same." By this time I had scooted my body closer to the German. Close enough to deliver an elbow to his ribs as the Afghan turned away; he got the message. In between coughs I changed the conversation. I said that now that we had settled on a price we would leave and bring the money back. I was not sure we had reached an agreement, but I just wanted to get the hell out of there before Khan started thinking about his observations. We left and I gave the arrest signal to the waiting Ministry of Justice officials. They made a pretty good haul. I really didn't care at that point.

Irene and three of the four kids left Kabul for the States the second week of July. To make the trip easier on Irene, Sean, age eleven, stayed with me. I had to go through Ankara and check out of the Regional Office. It would be some time before the new agent would arrive and they wanted me to bring any sensitive documents to Ankara for safekeeping. We were due to leave on the nineteenth. This all changed on the morning of July 17. Earlier in the night, I had heard muffled explosions, but had not given them much thought. But at dawn, the roar of Afghan Air Force MIG fighter jets came over the house. We had never experienced this before in Kabul. We then heard, saw and felt the reverberations of the rockets and machine gun fire from the aircraft. Most of the action appeared be in the vicinity of the Royal Palace, about two miles from our house, but some strafing came back our way. It was not difficult to figure out that a coup d'état was taking place.

King Zahir and his family had left Kabul several days before to obtain medical treatment in Rome. We were to learn that his cousin, Daoud Khan, had engineered the coup. I decided that we were better off at the Embassy than in our house. I put Sean in the Land Cruiser and pulled out into the street. I got out of the vehicle and closed the gate. As I did, I noticed several jeep type vehicles parked in front of the gate of the compound next to ours. I knew the owner was an Afghan Air Force General. I did not really know him, but we had exchanged greetings from time to time. As I reentered my Land Cruiser, I saw men in Army uniforms dragging the general out his gate. They shoved him roughly against the wall face first. All but one of the men stepped back. The other raised a pistol and shot the General twice in the back of the head. I accelerated around them and headed for the Embassy. This was not looking good. Fortunately Sean had not seen the shooting, but asked about the shots. I must have mumbled some explanation.

Things were pretty hectic at the Embassy and remained so throughout the day. The Marine Guards were on full alert, but they actually had little firepower. Just the same six shot revolvers I had carried in Rome as a Marine Guard fifteen years before. They approached me to borrow one of my shotguns. One of the Marines confided that they had literally, but unwittingly, participated in the start of the coup. They had been drinking beer at the Marine House sometime after midnight with the teenage son of the USAID Director. Several Afghan Army tanks had appeared at their gate and the Marines and teen had run out of the house to see what was going on. One of the tank crew had asked them where the Ministry of Defense was. The teenager, who spoke decent Farsi, gave directions and off rumbled the tanks. Back they came a short while later, still lost. They asked again for directions and the teenager repeated the instructions. Off they went again.......and back they came. This time they told the teen to get on the tank and take them to the Ministry. How often does a kid get to ride a tank? Off they went. When they arrived opposite the Ministry a short distance away, the tanks stopped. The tank crew chief told the teen to get off. They then turned their turrets and started blasting rounds into the Ministry building. That was the actual start of the coup. It was one scared kid who ran all the way back to the Marine House.

Those of us who had come to the Embassy spent the day making calls to get a head count of the Embassy staff and their families. The Ambassador arrived under police escort and held a hurried Country Team meeting. The Ambassador said that there was only one viable emergency road route for evacuation. That was via the Kabul Gorge, the Khyber Pass and on to Pakistan (the same tragic route the British had followed in 1892). My sense was that there had not been much contingency planning. The Embassy's security was the responsibility of the Administrative Officer, but that was only one of his many responsibilities. Ambassador

Neumann turned to me and asked if I would be willing to drive the route east. He wanted me to go at least to the Kabul Gorge to determine if the road was open. I wasn't crazy about the idea, but I said yes. Agent Mike Holm was back in the States for an extended period, so I'd have to do it alone.

I went to the Embassy garage under the building. I helped myself to a set of "CD" or "Corps Diplomatic" license plates. I replaced the standard Afghan plates I had on my Land Cruiser for the CD plates. I made sure I had my diplomatic passport and my 9mm pistol. I left Sean in the care of one of the Embassy secretaries and headed east. There was a lot of tank and armored car activity on the road. Most of it was headed into the city from the military base east of Kabul. As I got further though, I was shocked to see all the tanks that were off the road. There were a number of tanks in the ditch or turned turtle in a field. This was usually next to a curve. The tanks must have been rushing to Kabul from the base during the night. Not having driving lights on them, they apparently ran into problems navigating the curves.

I knew the Army base was just ahead. I slowed and took my pistol from my waistband and slid it under me. I came around a curve and slammed on the brakes in front of a road block of tanks and other armored vehicles. There were many soldiers with Kalashnikovs pointed at me. Two of them approached, looking menacing. They asked for cigarettes. Ah, I knew I had forgotten the most important item to have to get-yourself-out-of-a jam with. I showed them empty hands; no cigarettes. They were peering into the vehicle when an officer approached. I said hello and offered him my diplomatic passport. I didn't look much like a diplomat in Levis. The officer asked what I was doing there and where was I going. The easiest story to remember is the truth, so I told him I was scouting the route for the American Ambassador who was concerned that we might have to evacuate American personnel because of the coup. The officer was quite gracious. He assured me that everything was under control. There would be no need for an evacuation. If the situation worsened, I should come to see him and he would provide assistance. I took his name and thanked him. I turned around and got out of there. It was just in time, as that pistol was getting very uncomfortable under me.

It was almost evening when I returned to the Embassy. I reported the results of my trip to Ambassador Neumann, who was concerned that the road was blocked. He was heartened though that there was a professional officer running that operation. I grabbed Sean and headed home. I drove around the first turn past the Embassy and saw that the empty field to the side of the Embassy had been turned into a parking lot for tanks. There were dozens of them.

I took a quick photo. A short distance past them was the residence of the Defense Minister. As we approached it, several young soldiers ran into the street, knelt and aimed their Kalashnikovs at us. I stopped and they approached the vehicle and ordered us out. Someone had given Sean a small watermelon that he was holding. One soldier started jabbing at him and the watermelon with the muzzle of his weapon. I told the soldier to stop, but he ignored me. The eleven year old was not about to give up his prize, but he did so however, at my instruction. The soldiers were just young kids themselves, but they had the big guns. After my return from checking the road I had scrounged a few packs of cigarettes, so I told the soldiers I had cigarettes in the Land Cruiser. They kept their weapons trained on Sean and me as I retrieved the packs. The cigarettes did the trick and they released us.

Sean was quite unhappy about losing his melon and said so as we drove a few blocks further. We stopped at what was known as the Blue Mosque intersection. The name referenced the bright blue tiles that adorned the mosque on the corner. Here, the, now long-gone German police advisor had installed the only four way stop light in Afghanistan; and I had caught the red light. They say that distraction is the key to getting a kid's mind off of something. A Soviet tank with Afghan markings straddled the corner of the intersection opposite us. Sean fell silent;

staring. We were the only civilian vehicle on the road. The turret of the tank had been pointed down the street to our right. Now, it slowly pivoted until the barrel was directly in line with us. The barrel of its gun then lowered until we were staring right down it from 50 feet away. The crew was out of sight, "buttoned up" inside the tank. My first instinct was to accelerate across the intersection. I then thought what a waste it would be to have been blown away for running a red light. So I sat, mumbling curses directed at the German advisor. I was also hoping they hadn't issued the tank crews ammunition. Finally the light changed and I slowly preceded forward, the tank tracking us. We got past the limit of the tank's turret swing and I gunned it hard and headed home.

The next day, I thought I would visit Samad Azhar at the airport. I was hoping that my friend would be able to give me some idea of who was behind the coup and what was expected to take place. At the airport, however, I learned that Azhar was not there. His Deputy informed me that Azhar had just been appointed as the Chief of Staff to the new Minister of Interior. He was at his new office at the Ministry in central Kabul. At my request, the Deputy called Azhar. He told him that I wished to meet with him and Azhar agreed. Be very careful", the Deputy warned, "there are big problems." "Don't act like you and Azhar are friends," he cautioned.

I drove through the streets to the Interior Ministry where policemen there seemed to be running in every direction. I was ushered to the dreary office formally the domain of General Hakkim. Azhar was seated behind a desk going through file folders and speaking to several men. He looked up at me as though we had never met; I got the signal. I told him that I just wished for his office to know that I had completed my tour in Afghanistan. I would be leaving Kabul soon. I wanted to wish the Afghan Police good luck under the new government. Azhar thanked me politely and wished me a safe journey. He stood and we shook hands; all very formal.

Kabul calmed down somewhat over the next two weeks. It was clear that most of the Afghan authorities I had dealt with were no longer in their former positions. There was no reason to stay around any longer. I said my goodbyes inside the Embassy. Where I could, I said good-bye and thanks around Kabul to those who had helped me over the past two years. Leaving was bitter sweet. There had been many frustrations as expressed in this book. At the same time, new, lasting friendships had been made and I had the opportunity to work with outstanding colleagues in the Embassy, including Ambassador Neumann, Richard Schenck, and Sam Rickard. I had even had the opportunity to work with two Soviet professionals towards a common good.

Terrence M. Burke

Over the decades that have followed my Afghanistan tour, I often paused to wonder what had happened to my friend and Afghan Police colleague, Captain Abdul Samad Azhar. I could not imagine that he could have survived the PDPA coup d'état of 1978, the Soviet invasion of 1979, or the rise of the Taliban and the battles of the war lords. In conducting my research for this book, I was surprised to learn that he had survived. His story is a most dramatic one.

My sources for the description below of Azhar's post 1973 career were two-fold. First, a brief biography in "The Historical Dictionary of Afghanistan", by Ludwig W. Adamec of the University of Arizona at Tucson. The second source was a most remarkable one. It was a March 16, 2009, letter written by Azhar himself to the Woodrow Wilson International Center for Scholars in Washington, D.C. The Center had published a study titled "The KGB in Afghanistan", by Vasily Mitrokhin. Upon reading the study, Azhar apparently became highly incensed because the author named Azhar as the assassin of Afghan President Daoud. Azhar's letter was a detailed description of his professional and personal ordeal over 17 years. He vehemently denied any involvement in Daoud's death. (It is noted that most historians attribute Daoud's assassination to a small band of extremist Afghan Army Officers).

Following the 1978 Communist Coup, Azhar lost his

position with the Afghan Police and was jobless. Azhar was arrested by the ruling Khalq faction of the Communist Party and taken to Pule-Charkhi Prison where he was "treated badly". Fortunately, members of his wing of the Parcham Communist Party reacted against his arrest and he was released the next day.

Azhar was ordered to remain under house arrest by Hafizullah Amin, the head of the Khalq Party. He could walk only to a nearby market and then, only under the control of security guards. He was often taken to the office of the General Commander of Police where the Commander of the Police and the head of the secret police (AGSA) berated him and made threats against him.

In 1979, Azhar was kidnapped on his way to the market and taken to the AGSA headquarters. For ten days he was tortured. Then he was taken to the horrors of the Pule-Charkhi Prison to suffer and see what Azhar described as unbelievable atrocities. He was held until 1980 when he was released following the downfall of the Amin regime. He was named as General Commander of Police under the new government, but was dismissed following a disagreement with the Minister of Interior. Again, he was without a job.

In 1981, he was reinstated and was appointed Chief of the South-West Zone (southwest Afghanistan). There, he had serious disagreements with the Soviet advisers. He could not tolerate the blind bombardments and brutalities of their army against the civilians. A letter that he wrote to the party and government leaders in Kabul and local Soviet Military officials expressing his strong opposition to the Soviet tactics soon cost him his job. Again he was jobless, until 1983 when the Government started using ambassadorial assignments as a way to get dissenters out of Afghanistan. Azhar's first posting was as Ambassador to Cuba and then, from 1986–1989, he was Afghanistan's Ambassador to India. His term there ended abruptly when he challenged the "shameful" activities of the embassy's chief of secret intelligence. Azhar was briefly transferred to be Ambassador to Belgrade, but was dismissed in 1990 and returned to Kabul, jobless once again. I am currently attempting to contact him to determine his fate over the past 24 years.

There has been a horrendous loss of life and unimaginable tragedy in Afghanistan in the forty years since I served there. I only wish that the leaders of the former Soviet Union, the United States and of our Allies could have heard and considered the counsel Samad Azhar gave me on October 21, 1972:

> "The United States is trying to do something which has never been done successfully by any foreigner. That is to convince Afghans that it is for their own good to act against their own."

Azhar's advice was sound then and it is still sound today. Perhaps there would not have been as many human casualties and the multi billions spent, if the leaders had stopped to listen to history.

Epilogue

SEAN AND I LEFT KABUL and made quick stops in Ankara and Germany. We got to take the first 747 aircraft to fly from London to Boston. When we touched down in Boston, the overhead bins burst open. They dumped their contents on all of us. We then waited three hours for our luggage as the off load system couldn't handle the big aircraft. A fitting end to our Afghan tour, I thought. Irene and family had met us at the airport. I couldn't wait for Sean and me to tell them our stories of the bombings, the tanks, the road blocks and the soldiers pushing Sean around with their guns. Someone asked Sean how our last weeks in Kabul had been. "Boring," declared the eleven year old.

I was on an assignment in DEA Headquarters at the end of 1974 when I received a cable from the U.S. Embassy in New Delhi. The defendants in my India to Los Angeles smuggling case of 1972, Khan and Raj, were finally going to be tried for that crime. The Indian authorities wanted me there as a witness. I wasn't keen about returning to New Delhi given their attempt to permanently remove me as a witness shortly after their arrest. I had no choice though. I arrived there on January 8, 1975. For a week I stood in a small, concrete walled courtroom that had no heating system; and it gets cold in Delhi in January. The presiding magistrate, a Sikh, sat behind a counter that separated him from the rest of the room. At the other end of the counter was a chubby male court clerk. His "recording device" was an old manual typewriter. As the witness, I stood in front of the counter with the prosecutor and the defense attorney. About a dozen raggedly dressed prisoners, including Raj and Khan, sat shackled together on the cold concrete floor. Three or four guards paced around them. If a prisoner made a movement or whispered to another prisoner, a guard would reach across and whack him with his stave. Khan no longer weighed over 300 pounds and Raj no longer looked trim and athletic. They did not attempt to greet me.

My first day of testimony was on Friday. I then resumed my testimony the following Monday, Tuesday, and Wednesday. The testimony was unlike that given in a U.S. Court. The defense attorney would direct his question to the Magistrate. The Magistrate would then ask the attorney a question or two and then turn to me. He would ask me a question that sometimes reflected the question that had been asked by the defense attorney; but often it did not. I would answer the question. The magistrate would then turn to the court reporter and dictate a not always accurate version of my answer. The Magistrate would often have to repeat himself as the court clerk was usually reshuffling carbon paper between the seven sheets of bond that he would slowly wind into his typewriter. He seemed to only type a few lines before removing the paper and carbons and carefully placing the bond in seven neat piles. It was maddening!

Between the Friday, Monday, Tuesday and Wednesday testimony I had the weekend free. I was a bit paranoid and kept changing hotels in case the defendants renewed their effort to eliminate the witness. On Monday, I learned from the prosecutor that the Indian Customs authorities had not been briefed on my undercover role by the CBI and they had not known the judges had approved my leaving the country with the suitcase of drugs. They could well have arrested me at the airport and there had been no CBI officers there who could have assisted me. Over the next two days the defense strategy became very clear. Their bid to the court was that the judges who had examined and marked the drug evidence at the Embassy did not have the authority to allow me to leave the country with the drugs. Late on Wednesday afternoon, they sprung their trap. They presented the Magistrate with a written motion to have me arrested immediately for having taken drugs from India without legal authority. The prosecutor stood mute.

I stood dumbfounded. I took a long look at the prisoners on the floor. I might be joining their ranks shortly. I no longer had a diplomatic passport to protect me. I requested permission to address the Magistrate. I reminded him that I had traveled all the way to India from the United States to assist the court. I had stood before him for four days without complaint and had answered all questions truthfully. Given the abrupt nature of the defense motion, I was requesting that he not rule on the motion until the next day. I told him that I wished to meet with U.S. Embassy officials and seek their guidance. I felt I was not receiving adequate support from the prosecutor. The Magistrate granted my request and adjourned the court for the day.

I made a quick stop at my hotel, checked out, and headed for the Embassy. I did not ask, but I told them what I was going to do. I requested and received an Embassy car and driver to take me to the airport. At midnight, I was on yet another Pan Am 001 flight heading west from New Delhi. It took 10 months for the Embassy to obtain a ruling from the court that I had not broken any law in leaving India with the drugs. The judges had the authority to allow me to do so. They also received a written statement from the court that I would not be arrested. The bad news was that they wanted me back for more testimony.

On October 26, 1975, I returned. I was in the same courtroom, but with different Magistrate. This one was sharp and efficient. Raj and Khan were there on the floor. It had obviously been a difficult ten months for them and I felt sorry for them. This time my testimony was limited to two days. Raj and Khan were declared guilty. The guards gave them each a few whacks as they ushered them from the courtroom. My flight was scheduled to leave that night at midnight, but there were mechanical problems. At nine the next morning they announced that the mechanical problem had been fixed, but now the crew had to have eight hours rest. We had gone through security the night before, but were told we had to leave the international boarding area and return again that night. Two American "traveler type" couples protested and said they wanted to stay in the departure area. One woman appeared to be pregnant. They were obviously upset when they were informed they could not remain in place. They had made it through security and customs once and did not like risking a second chance, I thought to myself.

I went to the Embassy and "crashed" on a friend's couch in the residential apartments. That night I saw that the "travelers" had made it back through customs and security. They were very jubilant in the departure lounge. Once airborne, the Captain announced that the drinks were on Pan Am as an apology for the 24 hour delay. I was standing in the galley chatting with a couple of the cabin crew when a male member of the "travelers" staggered in. He had obviously taken the Captain up on his offer. I started a casual conversation with him. I asked him why he and his friends had protested so strongly when he wasn't allowed to spend the day in the departure area. Was it because the one lady was pregnant? He answered by giving us a big grin and pulling up the leg of his baggy pants. His legs were covered with long wraps of gauze. He peeled one off and removed a beautiful miniature Indian artifact. He proudly announced that he had many more strapped to him as did his companions. In fact, he told us, the girl with him was not actually pregnant. She had a statute strapped to her stomach inside a round foam pad.

I inquired as to how often they made such trips and he said at least every other month. I then asked if it was lucrative. "Not as lucrative as what I used to smuggle," he said. He went on to tell the stewardesses and me that he had been smuggling hashish from Afghanistan for several years. That had really been a moneymaker, he claimed. One of the stewardesses asked him why he had stopped. "Some bastard American "nark" named Terry Burke had gone to Kabul, gotten a lot of people arrested, and screwed up the business," he declared. He then stumbled back to his seat.

The stewardess glanced at her aircraft seating chart, "Aren't you Terry Burke?" she asked. When I told her I was, she asked me if the man had not made me angry. I told her that I didn't get angry, I got even. At my request, she gave me the "travelers'" names, dates of birth, and passport numbers from the plane's manifest. I walked back to my seat thinking I'd pass the information on in a message to CBI Inspector Singh. I was certain that the group's next time through Indian Customs would not be an easy one.

It had taken me two years to find out, but at least it now appeared that I had accomplished something while in Kabul.

Terrence Burke

About the Author

TERRENCE M. BURKE HEADS T. M. Burke International LLC., which he formed in 2001. Burke's private investigative career followed 30 years of law enforcement, intelligence and national security experience with the U.S. Marine Corps, The CIA and DEA. Burke's government service included extensive international assignments in Western Europe, the Middle East, Asia and Latin America.

From 1960 to 1970, Burke was a CIA intelligence operations officer, based primarily in Southeast Asia. In 1965, he was awarded the CIA Intelligence Star for Valor.

From 1970–1989, Burke held foreign and domestic positions at DEA including Kabul, Afghanistan, The Hague, Netherlands, Denver, Phoenix, and Chief of DEA's intelligence and enforcement operations in Washington DC.

From 1989 to 1991, Burke was Deputy Administrator of the DEA, and concurrently served as Acting Administrator. Burke regularly testified before Congress and appeared frequently on national and international television networks.

From 1994 to 2002, Burke was a member of the Alpine Rescue Team, participating in hundreds of technical rescues and searches in the mountains of Colorado.

In 2012, Burke published "Stories From The Secret War", an account of his tour in Laos with the CIA. There, he engaged in CIA's operations with the Hmong Hill Tribe in combat against North Vietnamese invaders. The book is available in printed, Kindle, and audio book format at LaPlataBooks.com or from your bookseller.